Praise for *The Side-Yard Superhero*

"*The Side-Yard Superhero* illustrates how we unexpectedly discover heroic qualities in our most ordinary daily acquaintances."

> —Dale Bumpers
> U.S. Senator from Arkansas (1975–1999)
> Author of *The Best Lawyer in a One Lawyer Town*

"You will laugh, you will cry, you will remember, and you will thank Rick Niece for re-opening a window to your childhood."

> —E. Kearney Dietz
> President, Arkansas Independent Colleges and Universities

"*The Side-Yard Superhero* floats back to an age of innocence and simplicity, nostalgically remembering a treasured friendship between two very different boys. A delightful read!"

> —Nancy Dane
> Author of *Where the Road Begins*

"Rick Niece vividly describes the charms of small-town America, where neighborly friendships develop character, attitude, and our responsibility to others."

> —Dr. David L. Warren
> President, National Association of Independent Colleges and Universities

"Welcome to DeGraff, Ohio. You will love our town and envy Rick's memories."

> —Philip Fawcett
> Mayor of DeGraff

"With a lyrical ability to retrieve carefully pocketed memories, Rick Niece reaches across generations to touch every heart."

> —Joey Halinski
> Advisory Board Member, The National Museum of Women in the Arts

"*The Side-Yard Superhero* encourages us to reconnect with the unique faces and places that make childhood worth remembering."

> —Steve Houchin
> Rick's boyhood friend
> Managing Partner, International Leadership Associates

THE SIDE-YARD
SUPERHERO

For the treasure
of memories.

Rick Niece

THE SIDE-YARD
SUPERHERO

BOOK ONE IN THE TRILOGY
LIFE IN DeGRAFF: AN AUTOMYTHOGRAPHY

Rick D. Niece

Synergy Books

The Side-Yard Superhero
Book One in the Trilogy
Life in DeGraff: An Automythography
Published by Synergy Books
P.O. Box 80107
Austin, Texas 78758

For more information about our books, please write to us, call 512.478.2028, or visit our website at www.synergybooks.net.

Publisher's Cataloging-in-Publication
(Provided by Quality Books, Inc.)

Niece, Rick D.
    Life in DeGraff, an automythography. Book one in the trilogy, The side-yard superhero / Rick D. Niece.
    p. cm.
    LCCN 2008928396
    ISBN-13: 978-0-9815462-0-9
    ISBN-10: 0-9815462-0-X

    1. Niece, Rick D.--Childhood and youth. 2. De Graff (Ohio)--Biography. 3. Friendship in children.
4. University of the Ozarks--Presidents--Biography.
5. College presidents--Arkansas--Clarksville--Biography.
I. Title. II. Title: Life in De Graff, an automythography. III. Title: Side-yard superhero.

F496.4.N54A3 2008   977.1'043'092
                           QBI08-600153

Author photo credited to Vinnie Tran.

This book is written with the intent of being as accurate as possible. It is based upon how the author remembers events and experiences.

10 9 8 7 6 5 4 3 2

Table of Contents

Automythography

A work of nonfiction that looks reflectively at what we think we remember and how we think we remember it; an iridescent memory based upon truth and fact.

R.D.N.

Prologue

Who Knows Why?

Who knows why
    we remember what we remember?
    Forget what we forget?
    Keep what we keep?
Who knows why
    the sight of kids playing catch
    takes me back to an all-dirt infield
    where Little Leaguers in rubber cleats
    use wooden bats with necessary trademarks?
Who knows why
    the grease-splattered scent of chicken frying
    takes me back to my grandmother's kitchen,
    crisping legs and wings oiling paper towels
    while cooling on the countertop
    through a churchless Sunday morning?
Who knows why
    a dozen orchestrated notes from "A Summer Place"
    take me back to a high school gym dance
    and my first touch of a virgin velvet dress
    pressed innocently against
    my Penny's new blue blazer?

Who knows why
    the rhythmic stroking
    of a sleek dog's slender flank
    takes me back to bicycle rides
    down rural county roads
    or along small town sidewalks
    where anxious front porches
    await their daily newspaper?
I know why.
At birth we are divided
    into two groups
    and assigned our roles.
In one group are
    the designated memory makers.
In the other are the memory keepers,
    my favorite.
Memory keepers
always know why.

I

A Late Night Wake-Up Call

Calls at 12:36 a.m. are seldom good news. While trying to sound like I was awake anyway, I managed a not-too-convincing hello. When I heard my mother's excited voice at the other end, I immediately began a mental inventory of potential tragedies. My mother is the family clearinghouse for death and serious illness, and she reports in earnest.

"Honey, are you awake?"

"What happened, Mom? Is everyone all right?"

"I know where Bernie Jones is," she said, ignoring my concern. "I tried to call you earlier. Why aren't you using the answering machine we bought you last Christmas?" Since my parents' retirement to Arizona, my mother often forgets the time difference between Arizona and Arkansas. I touched Sherée on the shoulder to let her know everything was okay, but she was still asleep.

"Bernie Jones," I answered quietly. "You know where Bernie Jones is?"

"Yes, Jinny Knief telephoned me about him. He's at the Heartland Nursing Home in Lakeview. I knew you'd want to know right away."

In rapid succession and no particular order, a montage of childhood scenes darted blurrily through the darkened bedroom like telephone poles outside the window of a school bus on its rural route. The scenes, hard to separate, were in the room with me. Some included Bernie, while others were simply fragments of people, places, and times in DeGraff so many years ago. And once memories like that begin, they carry the momentum of an Ohio State fullback and are difficult to stop.

"Honey," my mom interrupted, "are you still there?"

"Yes, Mom, thanks for calling. I'll talk to you tomorrow."

My mother rarely picks up on my exit lines.

"I knew you'd want to know about Bernie. Do you think you'll visit him when you're back in Ohio for the wedding? I don't believe there's anyone in Bernie's family still living, and I doubt he has any friends left."

"I know. I want to see him again. I've been thinking about him a lot recently." I drifted again to the scenes passing in front of me. I tried to slow them down but could not, and they played just out of reach.

"Are you still there?"

"Yes, Mom, I'm still here. Listen, I will call you tomorrow, I promise. I have a big day ahead of me and need to get back to sleep. Love you, good night."

At 3:03 a.m. I was still awake—digital clocks are a curse of exactness—thinking about Bernie Jones and my life in DeGraff. I felt overwhelmed by the memories and the thought that I'd soon be back in Ohio for my cousin's wedding. I hadn't returned in years. I started to cry like a kid, but gently and internally, and I'm not certain if I felt sad or happy, a blended sadappy.

I kept my promise the next day and called my mother. I like keeping promises, and I assured her I'd see Bernie when I was back in Ohio. That was another promise, made a long time ago, I wanted to keep as well.

The Ohio trip had to be brief because I needed to be back on campus Monday evening. Sherée had a weekend fundraising event in Little Rock and couldn't travel with me. I do not like traveling alone. But once I'd arrived, after managing the airports on my own, I'd be okay. My aunt and uncle in Lima invited me to stay with them, and I was looking forward to spending time with them and my cousins. I was sorry I wouldn't have time for Jinny Knief, our next-door neighbor during my years in

DeGraff and the sweetest lady I've ever known, but I couldn't see her this trip. That visit would be saved for my next return.

My flight was scheduled to land in Columbus on Friday afternoon, and with a rental car I'd be in Lima in time for the evening rehearsal dinner. The wedding was Saturday, and Sunday I'd visit Bernie in the nursing home, then return to Arkansas on Monday. It was a quick trip, but all in all my plan was a good one. Actually, the plan was a great one. After more than forty years, I was going to see Bernie Jones again.

II

Small Towns Have No Secrets

DeGraff is one of those barely visible midwestern towns travelers pass through but hardly notice. It's the kind of place that during the ninety-second drive through, people wonder aloud, "Who'd want to live here?" while secretly answering, "Me, maybe." That is, if they even noticed they were passing through.

When we moved from Oberlin, Ohio, DeGraff's population was a quaint 900. My guess is that several decades later, the town remains quaint and still one hundred short of a grand. But DeGraff overcompensated by being grand in other ways.

My dad attended college in Oberlin after his hitch in the Navy during World War II and, benefiting from the G.I. Bill, graduated from the Oberlin Conservatory of Music with a major in piano and minors in everything else instrumental and vocal. The offer to teach music, grades one through twelve, in a rustic one-building school district lured him and his family to DeGraff.

There were four of us: Dad, Mom, my younger brother Jeff, and me. The move was easy for my parents because they were both originally from that part of Ohio and anxious to return to small-town living. My brother and I didn't have a vote but went along for the ride. Hometowns become hometowns in very serendipitous ways. My youngest brother, Kurt, was born after we'd lived in DeGraff for five years and is the only true native.

I was four when we moved to DeGraff, and we lived there for sixteen years. In the minds of most townspeople, however, we were forever "new to the area." If you were not born, raised, and predicted to die in DeGraff, you were eternally a newcomer. Since we moved away after sixteen years, during my sophomore year at Ohio State University, I guess they were right. By their standards, we were short-termers.

I was a typical kid in a typical small town, if you can remain typical while your father is the school's only music teacher and the superintendent lives across the street. I think I was typical, but in a specimen under the microscope, "don't embarrass your father in front of the superintendent or the other teachers" kind of way. I usually listened and managed to avoid serious trouble.

A newspaper route was the first true love of my life. With my faithful sleek-flanked Dalmatian companion, Lady, gliding stride by stride beside my bright red, twenty-four-inch Huffy, I raced the streets and sidewalks of DeGraff to deliver newspapers, perfectly pitching the hand-rolled papers onto patiently waiting front porches. If delivering newspapers had been an Olympic event, I might have qualified as DeGraff's first medal recipient, Lady sharing the platform with me.

Life in DeGraff was as perfect as any boy could ask for. And DeGraff was home to Bernie Jones.

I took over Billy Neal's paper route when I was nine. Billy lived a street over from us and was one of the big guys I admired, but he never cared much for me. I was dependable and eager to start a career, while Billy was quasi-dependable and eager to get out of his.

His last day as a paperboy was on a Saturday, and he took me with him door-to-door as he collected thirty cents for the week of daily newspapers, the only time he showed me the collection process. Later that afternoon I bicycled along with him as he delivered the papers, but Monday I was on my own.

At our first collection stop, Bob and Janet Hall's house, Billy rang the doorbell several times and even knocked on the door, but no one answered. Wanting to be helpful, I went over to one of the front windows and peeked inside, trying to see if anyone was hiding behind a sofa or a lamp. That happened in our house if either of my parents was avoiding someone at the door. The next thing I knew, Billy cracked me on the side of the head and hollered, "What are you doing, you little jerk? Never peep into a customer's window! Do you want to get us arrested or something?"

I'm forever thankful to Billy for deterring me from a life of crime as a peeping Rickie, and I never looked into another customer's window. Of course I didn't want to get arrested, and who knew what Billy's unspecified "something" might involve?

Along the rest of our collections, in typical teenage boy style, Billy explained that most of the customers were fairly normal, at least by DeGraff standards, except for three. He warned me that Fern Burdette was a crazy old lady who'd talk your leg off if you let her. Laughing, he added that was probably how she'd lost hers. Then shaking his head like someone who'd heard about the sad details of her life story but didn't care, he smirked that Miss Lizzie Moore was a reclusive spinster who might as well have been a hermit. Finally, in almost a whisper, an odd volume for Billy Neal, he said Bernie Jones was also on the route. He then declared that was all he was going to tell me.

It didn't matter. I thought I already knew all there was to know about the three of them, especially Bernie Jones. Small towns have no secrets and little hesitation in sharing them.

DeGraff was divided into four zones for newspaper delivery, and to this day I still believe I had the choice route and best customers. Four of us delivered *The Bellefontaine Examiner*, a daily paper except for Sunday published in Bellefontaine, the county seat and largest city in Logan County. All four of us—John Slater and the Tamplin brothers, Charles and Herb—kept our routes for a long time. Other kids in DeGraff wanted our jobs, but we were not about to give them up, knowing we had a good thing. I had my route from age nine until I graduated from high school, and the others kept theirs for almost as long. We made ten cents a week per customer, and with my seventy-two customers the pay was good by DeGraff standards.

The newspapers were brought to DeGraff from Bellefontaine in a tired-looking Chevrolet pickup truck by a questionable character named Senior Junior. After Senior Junior delivered the two large bundles to the detached garage at Art Haugen's house, we'd count out the papers we each needed for our individual routes and talk man talk while folding the papers tightly for throwing onto porches. Senior Junior sometimes hung around to tell us about an older woman he was dating or what he'd already read in the paper during his trip to DeGraff, proud of his ability to drive and read at the same time.

I always liked Senior Junior and his unusual name, although I thought the name to be oxymoronic, like delicious liver, because Senior Junior was a sophomore when he dropped out of high school. I wish I'd asked him about his name and how he got it. During my freshman year in high school, he was killed in an accident between Bellefontaine and DeGraff while bringing us the papers. A bulk milk truck pulled out in front of him, and my guess is he was engrossed in reading the daily news and forgot to look up. The next day Senior Junior made the front page of *The Examiner*, and in adolescent logic we thought it was pretty ironic he couldn't read about himself. We also learned his real name was Milburn.

With a canvas bag of seventy-two folded newspapers slung over my right shoulder and weighing down my left side, I delivered the papers on my bicycle. I was an expert at riding fast and flinging the papers perfectly onto each porch as I sped by, leading porches better than a champion skeet shooter leads clay pigeons. Up and down hills, around sharp corners, within narrow alleyways, and through the center of town, I raced and threw, threw and raced. Most days my route took about an hour and a half, starting at 4:00 p.m. and ending around 5:30 p.m.

My customers knew I was approaching because of my loud melodic whistling. I loved to whistle, and no one seemed annoyed by it. Because of my musical upbringing, I usually whistled something classical. Beethoven, Tchaikovsky, and Rachmaninoff were standards in my puckered repertoire, but every now and then the latest Elvis, Everly Brothers, Lesley Gore, or Lettermen caught my fancy and joined the list.

I remember when I was about four or five and riding in the backseat of a car with my Uncle Robert and Aunt LaVelva, my Uncle Robert asked what I wanted to be when I grew up. He could really whistle and was able to perfectly imitate at least a dozen different birdcalls. I told him I was going to be a professional whistler and wanted to hire him to be my trainer. They both laughed, but I was serious.

Each day as I sped down the hill on Boggs Street, raced past the box factory—officially known as The Mid-State Container Corporation, and DeGraff's only major industry—and prepared for the bumps of the railroad tracks running through the middle of town, I'd make my whistle a little louder, stop it suddenly, then listen carefully for the excited voice from the side yard of the first house on the right after the tracks.

"Rickie, my boy, hurry up!" I think he waited all day every day, except Sundays, for me to deliver the paper. I liked all of my customers, but Bernie Jones was my favorite.

Bernie's dad was a rural mail carrier and his mom a housewife, but I seldom saw either of them. Occasionally when I'd deliver the paper, Bernie's mom would be hanging laundry in the backyard or taking it down. I don't remember ever seeing her smile, and I thought I knew the reason. Although Mr. Jones also seemed stoical, I did experience his anger one Saturday morning during my weekly collection for the paper. Bernie usually had the money jangling in his front shirt pocket and ready for me, but this Saturday his father made a point of paying me himself.

On holidays like Thanksgiving, Christmas, and the Fourth of July, a paper wasn't published. For those weeks the paper was officially a quarter instead of the usual thirty cents because it was delivered five days instead of the regular six. Most customers, without hesitation, paid me the thirty cents, and I'd carefully place the extra nickel in my left front pocket instead of slipping it into the nickel slot of the four-cylinder change maker attached to my belt. The metal changer held pennies, nickels, dimes, and quarters and was used for business purposes; my left front pocket was for bonus nickels. I looked forward to paperless holidays because by the time I finished collecting, my pocket bulged like David Downing's cheek when he had it stuffed full with Mail Pouch chewing tobacco. David worked at the DeGraff Stockyards and Meat Packing Company where, among the cattle and pigs, chewing tobacco was considered acceptable.

Two collection Saturdays after the Fourth of July, Bernie's dad met me at the front door before I had a chance to knock.

"Here's you a quarter," he said harshly.

My voice quavered. "But, Mr. Jones, the paper's thirty cents."

"You were paid thirty cents last week when it should've only been twenty-five. No paper on the Fourth of July, remember? You owe me a nickel. Do you take advantage of all of your customers like that?"

My brain went numb, and I couldn't think. I suddenly felt like one of the thieving boys working within Fagin's gang of orphans in *Oliver Twist*. They didn't know any better either, but at least I was clean, well fed, and had parents who cared about me.

"Most of my customers give me the extra nickel," I finally managed to mutter, eyes cast downward studying his shoes and mine. "I think they want me to have it."

"Then they're damn fools," he said, turning and closing the door.

I didn't see Bernie that morning, and he wasn't in the side yard when I delivered the paper later in the afternoon. I spent the rest of the weekend wondering if he was being punished for my five-cent transgression.

I'd never known anyone like Bernie Jones. I felt instinctively, as only a young boy can, that my delivering the paper was the high point of his day. And there were times he was the high point of mine. I couldn't spend a lot of time with Bernie because he was toward the beginning of my route, and I had customers waiting for their papers. Six o'clock was suppertime at our house, so I had a built-in deadline. But I knew whatever time I had for him was precious and appreciated.

Bernie was born with severe cerebral palsy and confined to a wheelchair.

SMALL TOWNS

Small towns are like
     an older brother,
     a favorite aunt and uncle,
     another set of parents
even when you are not orphaned.
And small towns do not mind being second.
Small towns raise you.
       They look after you.
         They nag at you
     in a positive way.
Small towns ask for nothing in return,
       in true unconditional love,
     when you return
no matter how many years later.
And even if you are both
     no longer what you were,
you are each as you should be
      remembered.

III

Bernie Jones

When Billy Neal told me that Bernie Jones was on the paper route, I was afraid of meeting him. Who knows why little kids fear what they fear? I was curious but, nonetheless, afraid. During Sunday supper the night before my first day to deliver papers, I asked Dad what to expect when I met Bernie. What should I say to him? How should I treat him? What could we talk about?

My dad, in logical *Father Knows Best* fashion, replied I should talk to Bernie like I talked to any of my friends. He then added, "Who knows? You may like him and become friends."

And we did become friends, even though our meeting on my first day to deliver his paper was anything but smooth. I'm still uncertain how either one of us survived that day to begin a friendship.

I stopped at the box factory parking lot, just before the railroad tracks, to catch my breath and my nerve. I could see Bernie in his wheelchair, and he seemed to be looking in my direction. I couldn't tell if he saw me because his head kept rolling back and forth, and I had a hard time following his eyes. But I had the feeling he knew I was close by and watching him.

After another minute, I swallowed a deep breath and coasted down the hill and over the tracks. When he saw me, his arms and legs windmilled. I parked my bike a few feet from him in the yard, reached for a paper, and froze. I could not move a muscle while every one of Bernie's seemed to be twitching asymmetrically. While Bernie was fast-forwarding, I was freeze-framed. This was not going well.

Bernie said something, but in a halting, guttural language I didn't understand.

"What?" I stammered.

Bernie garbled again, and I continued to stammer. We were in those moments equally inarticulate.

Finally, after at least half a dozen attempts, I understood his five words.

"Where's Billy? Who are you?"

"He quit! I'm Rickie! Gotta go!"

And that was it. I dropped the paper by his chair, jumped on my bike, and raced away. I don't remember delivering any of the other papers on the rest of my route, but I must have. We received only one telephone call that evening, from Jake Long—a customer I'd missed. But he was nice about it, and Dad drove me to his house. I do remember putting my head in Dad's lap and crying during our drive home. I do remember that.

Dad, God bless him, simply said I'd do better the next time I saw Bernie, and he gave me wonderful advice. He said not to become fixated on my own nervousness but to focus on making Bernie feel at ease with me. He then said he was proud of me, and I felt better even though I knew I'd done nothing to earn his pride.

The next day I didn't stop at the box factory, but raced over the railroad tracks and rode straight toward Bernie. I parked my bike, walked right up to him, and placed the newspaper on his lap. "Hi, I'm Rickie."

"Well, Rickie, my boy, I'm Bernie." He only had to say it twice before I understood. I was focused.

I reached out to shake his hand the way my Grandpa Jack had taught me with the words, "Shake hands like a man, not like a fish. Shake with a firm grasp. You can learn a lot about a man from his handshake."

But Bernie's hand was swinging around like the hand of a New York City traffic cop, and we never connected. Looking like I was swatting away a swarm of gnats, I would have settled for a fish shake.

I then asked an embarrassingly stupid question, a moronic and imbecilic question, the kind that hangs out there like a clothesline of irretrievable holey underwear.

"What do you like to play?"

Crap—what do you like to play? What do you like to play! At that moment I knew I was a simpleton, a nine-year-old half-wit. I was certain I'd live my entire life and never be full-witted. I decided right then and there that I was quitting the route after only my second day, figuring I could still build a respectable résumé out of "Former Newspaper Boy, Two Days Experience."

But Bernie laughed, and for the first time I saw his banana-skin yellow teeth. I'd been warned about his teeth, and they were a sight to behold.

I laughed back.

"Pretty stupid question, right?"

"Yeah, stupid question."

"What do you like, Bernie?"

"I like *Dick Tracy*."

This time I understood exactly what Bernie said, and at that moment our friendship began. I also liked *Dick Tracy*, cartoonist Chester Gould's ingenious creation. Our every late-afternoon newspaper delivery ritual began with me unfolding his paper and reading aloud the latest *Dick Tracy* comic strip. During our years of friendship, I grew into full-wittedness while reading a comic strip to a wheelchair-bound boy with cerebral palsy.

Except for his eyes, I don't think Bernie Jones had control over any part of his body. He was strapped into his wheelchair by a large leather belt wrapped around his middle and buckled at the back of the chair. When I'd pedal into sight, his arms would flail like the wings of a wounded turkey with legs kicking in the air, and he'd laugh a throaty laugh through his mouthful of corncob teeth.

"Rickie, my boy, where you been? What's going on with *Dick Tracy*? Is Sparkle in this one?"

Each afternoon before folding my papers in Haugen's garage, I'd quickly thumb through the pages to get to the section of black-and-white comics and *Dick Tracy*, the sixth panel down. I'd read the strip slowly for my own enlightenment and then practice it softly under my breath in preparation for reading to Bernie. I wanted to know what words to dramatically emphasize and when to sneak in extended pauses in order to get Bernie in full whirlybird motion. After teasing him with the long pauses, I'd anxiously anticipate his reaction, and he never let me down.

"Why'd you stop? Come on, Rickie, my boy, why'd you stop? Did something bad happen?"

This was during the dreaded Flattop Jr. story line. He was as evil as his vile father, Flattop Sr., who'd menaced our hero a couple of decades earlier. Bernie and I swore that Flattop Jr. was worse than his old man. Flattop haircuts were popular, especially among kids and teenagers. DeGraff's slightly delinquent James Dean imitators, like Bill Greg and Ronnie Walker, wore their flattops with Brylcreem varnished ducktails. Cecil Carr, the town barber, charged one dollar for regular haircuts and $1.25 for a flattop, but I figured with a nasty name like flattop the style wasn't worth the extra quarter, and I didn't want one even if Cecil cut it for free.

Bernie and I hated Flattop Jr. and cringed every time he got the better of Dick Tracy and his partner, Sam Catchem. Flattop Jr. became more and more villainous with each reading, his mockery of our hero frustrating us both. We both shamelessly rejoiced when Flattop Jr. was killed by policewoman Lizz Groove. Bernie's exuberance quickly turned to shock, however, when we learned during the elaborate plot finale that Flattop Jr.'s last name was Jones—Flattop Jones Jr. After I read the panel, Bernie sat almost motionless. Now, I'd never seen him motionless, but this time was pretty close. I nodded sympathetically to him, turned, and pedaled away to finish my route. We never uttered Flattop Jr.'s surname again.

I think Bernie had a crush on Sparkle Plenty, the beautifully shaped daughter of B.O. Plenty and his wife, Gravel Gertie. Whenever Sparkle appeared in one of the *Dick Tracy* strips, Bernie would ask me to reread it while showing him the illustrations. I'd then kid him, and he'd get embarrassed with ears turning maraschino cherry red while denying any romantic interest. But we both knew his fantasy.

Over the years, outside of his mom and dad, I think I was the only other person who fully understood Bernie's nearly incoherent speech patterns. He was extremely difficult to comprehend, and his voice had a croupy, gasping quality to it. But in the same way six-year-olds understand the fractured, inarticulate language of their two-year-old siblings, I understood Bernie. After a few weeks of friendship, I understood each word and every sentence perfectly. Communication became second nature between us.

Our afternoon routine seldom varied. After I'd read *Dick Tracy*, he'd ask about my day in school, wanting to know the best thing I had learned. Bernie never went to school, as this was well before special education or any other specialty training programs in DeGraff, so I was a primary source for his informal education. I think my eventual interest in teaching subconsciously began with Bernie.

Because he was intrigued by science and literature, whatever I was taking during a particular year in either subject became his mini-curriculum. I think he liked science because he wanted to know more about why things are as they are. He never asked me, but I believe he was searching for answers about himself and his condition. Although I never heard him complain, not once in all those years, I figured he was curious to find out if he or his parents had done something wrong. I didn't know and was of no help in that regard.

He enjoyed *Beowulf* during my junior year in English, and for several weeks after we finished reading it in class, he'd ask me to retell the story about Grendel and his mother. My Old English dialect was hardly authentic, but Bernie appreciated my efforts.

I remember one spring when I was in junior high, Bernie shared a wish of his that stayed with me for months after. Actually, it has stayed with me a lifetime. He mused, "You know what I wish, Rickie, my boy?" I shook my head. "I wish we had two-way wrist radios like Dick Tracy and Sam Catchem."

Brilliant Smith, the blind son of wealthy industrialist Diet Smith, invented the two-way wrist radio, Dick Tracy's most famous gadget. Every kid I knew dreamed about having a set.

"With a wrist radio," Bernie said, "I could listen when you're in class. I could hear everything myself."

At that moment I had a glimpse into Bernie's world and saw how hungry he was to be like other kids: to be able to study, to learn, and to go to school. While the rest of us complained about school, Bernie longed for it. And I longed for it for him. Several years later when Brilliant Smith invented the two-way wrist television, I imagined Bernie's ecstasy at the thought of us with televisions strapped to our wrists.

"Yeah, Bernie," I answered softly. "Wrist radios really would be something. Maybe someday we'll own a set."

We knew we never would, but in that moment of good friend wistfulness, his wish was hope enough for both of us. During the next couple of weeks, I listened extra carefully at school and appreciated being in class.

IV

Nothing Hidden

Fern Burdette's house was a few blocks before Bernie's. Billy Neal didn't like Fern, but she mesmerized me immediately. I never knew for certain if Fern thought of me as being a real friend, but I'd have been honored if she did. I'm not certain what I considered her to be. All I know is that she was fascinating, and no one in DeGraff was quite like her. Fern defined character in every sense of the word, and I still smile when I think about her.

Fern Burdette left DeGraff to become a newspaper journalist after graduating from DeGraff High School in 1904, which sounded like ancient history to me. She traveled the world on reporting assignments, and as a female reporter, she was a trendsetter. Entering a male-dominated occupation, being single, wearing a wooden leg, and spitting like a man made her out of place almost anywhere, but especially in DeGraff. Fern was our futuristic anachronism, and she relished the job.

After retiring from the newspaper business, Fern moved back to DeGraff. She liked that I was a paperboy, and she was proud we shared the newspaper business as our profession. She talked a lot about her days as a journalist and lamented how current editors and their papers had gone soft, burying real news on the back pages while using the front page for fluff. She'd routinely quote her first boss, the editor of a paper where she had apprenticed in Kansas City as a journalist. "Fern, never hide the news from your readers. Keep it right in front of them." And that's how Fern lived her life, with nothing hidden and everything up front.

I once asked why, with all the places to choose from, she had come back to DeGraff. "My life got too complicated, Rickie, and I needed to get away from that life and back to a snail's pace." She spit while chewing her ever-present wad of gum. "This is simple, and I like simple. Besides, DeGraff is about as lifeless as I could get while still breathing." I knew old Fern actually cared for DeGraff, but she never wanted anyone to know she had an ounce of sentimentality.

Fern was a trendsetter in another way as well, and it was a trendsetting difference boldly showing Fern Burdette was one woman well before her time in DeGraff or the entire Midwest. Fern wore a brassiere as her normal piece of outer clothing—no blouse, no shirt, no sweater, just a brassiere from the waist up. That was Fern, with nothing hidden and everything up front. She went shopping in downtown DeGraff that way, she paraded with her dog on long walks that way, she drove her wood-paneled station wagon around town that way, and she shared a portion of her Saturday mornings with me that way. If she was a scandal, no one had the nerve to tell her. If she was pornographic, I never thought of her like that. She was just Fern: brassiere showing, hard drinking, wooden leg walking, frequent spitting, world interesting Fern.

As far as I knew, Fern had only one true love in her life, and that was her well-trained, full-blooded Dalmatian, Duke, as beautiful a dog as I ever laid eyes on. My Lady, who accompanied me daily on the newspaper route, was also a Dalmatian, but she was part Greyhound and much thinner and sleeker in the flanks.

I enjoyed stopping at Fern's house when collecting for the paper and was consistent in my Saturday morning collection schedule, getting to Fern's about 10:00 a.m. She'd be sitting on her cluttered, veranda-type front porch in an old fabric-covered stuffed chair with major city newspapers strewn around her, Duke at her feet, and an extra glass of icy lemonade waiting for me on a small bench. She'd warn me not to get our lemonade glasses mixed up because mine was the only one containing just lemonade. The first time she made the comment and I didn't get it, she pointed to a bottle of Jack Daniels by her chair and said she could count on three things only: Duke, Jack, and me. I didn't mind being third. Our Saturday morning routines were always the same, except during the winter months when we'd have cups of hot tea instead of lemonade, again with her warning not to mix our cups.

Duke was one smart dog. I loved Lady, but she could only lift her right paw to shake hands no matter how hard I worked to train her. Fern's Duke could have starred on *The Ed Sullivan Show*. Fern would command, "Duke, how many pennies in a nickel?" and Duke would bark, bark, bark, bark, bark, and then, I swear on a Bible, the dog smiled.

"Duke, fetch me the *New York Times*." Duke would nuzzle his nose through the mound of papers surrounding Fern, paw out a *New York Times*, gently grip it in his mouth, and place it on Fern's lap. Not wanting to sound disrespectful, I never asked if it was the most recent issue.

Duke even paid me for Fern's weekly papers. "Duke, get Rickie's money," Fern would command and then sit up straight in her chair. Duke would stretch his head behind Fern's waist, grasp the envelope from Fern's back pocket, and bring it to me. The envelope was never drooly.

After Duke's tricks, Fern would wave him back to his rug. "Lie down, honey, the adults are going to talk now." Even though I was just a kid, Fern treated me like a grown-up. But before going to his rug, Duke always trotted over to Fern for an exchange. I never know how to explain the exchange without it sounding abnormal, but in all the years I knew Fern Burdette that exchange seemed as normal as snow in January. Fern would lean down toward Duke, Duke would lift his head, and Fern's wad of gum was dispassionately transferred from her mouth into his. Then flopping down on the rug in the corner of the porch, butt to butt with Lady, Duke contentedly chewed their gum. After our talk for the morning, Fern always requested the gum back, there'd be another exchange, and we'd say our good-byes. Gum must have kept its flavor longer in those days.

Much of what I know about journalism, the world, and eccentricity, I learned from Fern Burdette during our Saturday morning talks.

The conversations never lasted more than fifteen minutes, much like a Lowell Thomas newsreel, but they were my guides to foreign adventure. Fern told a story in a *Reader's Digest* condensed style, and her journalist background made the stories interesting and to the point.

One Saturday morning Fern met me at the sidewalk before I could walk to the porch, and I knew instantly something was wrong. "Don't come on the porch, Rickie. We lost Duke last night, and I got him laid out on his rug. I'm going to bury him in the backyard but wanted to tell you first."

"You need any help?" I squeaked, tears cascading down my cheeks and wetting my T-shirt. "Can I help, Fern?"

"No, Rickie," she said not looking at me, "this is one thing you're too young for. I'll take care of him myself." I left Fern alone with Duke.

I never saw Fern Burdette again. She wasn't on the porch when I delivered the paper that afternoon. I heard she'd driven herself to Mary Rutan Hospital in Bellefontaine and checked herself in. Fern had never been sick a day in her life, but she told the doctor she just was not feeling right. Dad was going to drive me to visit her on Wednesday, but she died in her sleep Tuesday night.

I remember hoping that heaven didn't have a dress code and allowed chewing gum and mathematical dogs.

V

The Thatcherville Hill Adventure

The boundaries of Bernie's life were extremely small. Although his house was on a street paralleling Main Street and the center of town, he didn't have much to look at. The multi-building box factory blocked Bernie's view of downtown. The two-story Carter house, boarding Mrs. Carter and her two adult children who still lived at home, was positioned directly across the street on a yard gone to seed. That was pretty much the visual extent of Bernie's side-yard worldview.

Miss Lizzie Moore lived beside Bernie. A strange and intriguing spinster, Miss Lizzie, as far as anyone could determine, never left her house. Her groceries and mail were delivered outside the front door, but I never saw her walk outside to get them. On the newspaper collection days she didn't want to be bothered, I'd find the money under the front doormat.

When she did come to the door, Miss Lizzie was always nice to me, and we'd have a conversation after she poked her arm around the slightly opened screen door to give me the change for her weekly paper. Occasionally, she'd ask how the crippled boy next door was doing, and I'd tell her Bernie was getting along fine, emphasizing his name. She didn't seem to catch onto my hints about his name, or didn't want to, and continued to refer to him as the crippled boy. I hated the term but didn't think she meant it in a truly disrespectful way.

Although Bernie's world was minimal, he did relish two characters: the fictional Dick Tracy and the fractional Flippo the Clown. I was able to keep him current on Dick Tracy, but with Flippo he was on his own. Flippo the Clown had a matinee movie television show primarily for kids from 3:00 p.m. to 4:00 p.m. every weekday. His program was broadcast from a station in Columbus, so Flippo was a clown of limited celebrity. Bernie loved Flippo's corny jokes, vaudeville routines, and slapstick squirt-water-in-your-eye-from-a-fake-lapel-flower gags. The movies were usually Andy Hardy, Henry Aldrich, Shirley Temple, Tarzan, or grade B horror flicks shown over a two- to three-day period, depending upon their length and Flippo's number of high jinks.

Before our daily *Dick Tracy* dose, Bernie would try to tell me one of Flippo's lame jokes and either laugh through the punch line or forget it. It didn't matter, though, because Bernie's telling of a joke was much better than the joke itself. If Flippo the Clown made Bernie feel good, he was all right by me.

Even though Bernie's world was confined, I never heard him complain, and that's why I tried to accommodate his periodic, sometimes illogical requests. Although most of his ideas defied reason, he did happen upon a plausible adventure every now and then. One time he decided he wanted me to take him around on my route as I collected from my customers, arguing that since I knew how he spent his time, he wanted to see firsthand how I spent some of mine.

For once I didn't dismiss his idea right away and told Bernie I'd consider it. It had possibilities, and as I thought through the logistics of having Bernie in tow, I came up with a plan. Since Bernie's house was about one-third the way into my route, backtracking with him made no sense, so the first third was out. The last third of the route was on the other side of town and involved the murderous Harshbarger Hill, my daily forty-five degree uphill exercise. Coming down Harshbarger Hill was a thrill but going up was a challenge. The two of us could never manage either up or down, so that eliminated the last third.

The middle third of the route—from Bernie's house on Boggs Street, to the south side of Main Street, and on to Thatcherville Hill—had possibilities. Thatcherville Hill was the third-steepest incline in DeGraff, with Harshbarger Hill being first and the hill on Mill Street beside our house a close second, but Thatcherville Hill was manageable. The middle of the paper route was perfect for Bernie.

When I explained my idea to him, he was a little miffed he'd not be experiencing the entire route but soon came around to liking the plan. He made me promise we'd use his wheelchair and not the wooden cart his dad had built for him several years before. When he was younger, Bernie's mom and dad pulled him up and down their street in the cart, but he was convinced he had outgrown it. I also think the cart embarrassed him, so I wasn't about to argue with him. We chose the next Saturday for our big adventure. Bernie got his mom's approval, and I ran it by my parents as well. Surprisingly, his mom agreed to let him go and even seemed pleased about our excursion.

I don't know if Bernie's mom was overly protective or not, but she definitely was protective and had a right to be. As a kid, even I understood her fears for his safety. Because of her cautious nature, most of Bernie's grand plans for us never saw a glimmer of sunshine.

Creeks and ponds were her biggest fear, so fishing was not an option no matter how hard Bernie begged. I didn't argue with Bernie's mother on his behalf, not even when he pleaded for me to. The image of a submerged Bernie strapped in his wheelchair made me a contented landlubber with a dry-docked Bernie.

As a result, Bernie's endlessly daydreamed adventures remained mostly unrealized musings, living alone with him within the narrow confines of a small side yard. But on a couple of rare occasions I was allowed to help Bernie escape, in safe passage, from his world into a new one. Thatcherville Hill was definitely a new world.

I had a few days to figure out our method of travel. At first I thought I might be able to rig up some type of apparatus to hook Bernie to my bike and pull him, but I quickly rejected that as being too cumbersome. Besides, I didn't have the required rigging. I knew that Israel Gross, DeGraff's last blacksmith, had a harness we could use, but I didn't like the picture of me pulling a harnessed Bernie. I'd look like I was trying to plow the sidewalks of DeGraff with him.

I finally decided simple was best. I'd leave my bike at Bernie's after collecting the first part of my route and push him house to house. I could then take him back to his house and finish the rest of the collections myself. The plan was workable, and I was pleased with myself for devising it.

I started my collections early that morning and arrived at Bernie's house about 9:00 a.m. He was sitting in the side yard with two paper bags and a thermos on his lap.

"What's that stuff?" I asked, clicking down the kickstand and parking by his chair.

"Peanut butter sandwiches and lemonade," he replied proudly. "Mom thought we might need provisions."

No way that would work. I was going to have my hands full on this trip anyway without having to stop every few feet to pick up the sandwiches and thermos bouncing off his lap.

"Bernie, we won't need that. Snacks from customers while collecting come with the territory."

I stuffed the sandwich bags and thermos behind the shrubs in front of their house, and the adventure began.

Our first stop was across the street at the Carters, and I pushed Bernie up the front sidewalk and knocked on the door. Mrs. Carter was expecting me and had her thirty cents ready. When she saw Bernie, she smiled and said good morning, figuring I had merely wheeled him from across the street for a different view. She didn't know her home was the first leg of our expedition, and I didn't tell her.

Next was Miss Lizzie Moore, and I had been worried about this stop. Bernie and I seldom talked about his condition, but I'm certain he didn't think of himself as being crippled.

Miss Lizzie came to the screen door and gave us both a quizzical look before addressing me. "Well, you have the boy from next door with you today." Even though she had lived by Bernie forever, she was meeting him for the first time.

"Yes, Miss Lizzie, this is Bernie Jones." She then did a remarkable thing: she squeezed herself sideways out the door to stand on the front porch beside us. Miss Lizzie looked different in the sunlight and out of the shadows of her door. Her skin was pink and porcelain, and she was dainty as a lawn statue.

"Very nice to meet you, Mr. Jones," she said with a slight curtsy, "I'm Lizzie." She reached out and caressed his forearm while handing me six nickels. "You gentlemen enjoy the rest of the day."

"Thanks, Miss Lizzie," was all I could manage before she squeezed herself back behind the screen door and quickly closed the front door.

As I pushed him across the street to the next customer, my friend Denny Allison's house, Bernie was smiling sunshine yellow. "Miss Lizzie was nice."

"Yes, she was, Bernie. You bring out the best in people."

Some of my customers, including Denny's parents, left their money in a *Bellefontaine Examiner* envelope hung from the doorknob, making the envelope stops routine. Seems funny by today's standards to think honesty and trust of that nature ever existed, but they did in DeGraff. I never once, in all my years of delivering newspapers, had money stolen.

After we left Bernie's world on Boggs Street and turned onto South Main, we were a couple of hundred yards from downtown DeGraff. Bernie asked me to stop pushing him, and he stared ahead at the two- and three-story brick and limestone buildings of DeGraff's business district like he was seeing them for the first time. Turns out, in a way, he was.

"I've never seen DeGraff like this. We drive through town in the car, but this is different. I like it."

Bernie's speech pattern was oftentimes agonizingly slow, and he struggled to finish long sentences. Verbalizing was a difficult process, and I tried to be patient and let him work through the words at his own pace without finishing his sentences for him, even if I thought I knew what he was going to say. Most of the time I was able to keep quiet until he finished.

"Yeah, it is a nice sight from here," I said, standing behind him, my hands caressing the back of his wheelchair. We shared the view for another minute, and then I suggested moving on because we had a long way to go.

A couple of my customers on South Main made a big fuss over Bernie. Bill Shoemaker, Mayor of DeGraff for two decades before he retired, was a great storyteller and joker. Years as a politician do that to you. He told Bernie that when he was younger, he'd watched Bernie's house being built by Bill Baseore and other carpenters from the DeGraff Lumber Company. He said it was the finest house on Boggs Street. After a perfectly timed pause, he said it was about the only house on Boggs Street at the time, and we laughed, especially Bernie. As we were leaving, Mr. Shoemaker told Bernie that his dad was a fine and honest man, and I thought that was a great thing for Bernie to hear. Bernie was pleased and thanked him with a wobbly nod of his head.

The Hostetlers lived across the street from the Shoemakers. Mrs. Hostetler was usually waiting each Saturday with a plate of warm, freshly baked chocolate chip cookies and a quart carton of cold milk, her front porch a nice place to take another break. The porch had several steps, too many for me to maneuver Bernie up, so Mrs. Hostetler and I carried down a couple of chairs and sat on either side of him. We lounged in the shade of a large sugar maple eating cookies and drinking cold milk. Like corporate executives, paperboys also have their perks.

As Mrs. Hostetler small talked about the beautiful day, her vegetable garden, and flower patches, she included Bernie in the conversation with questions like, "Bernie, do your parents have a garden?" and "What's your favorite kind of flower, Bernie?" I liked the way she involved him, but Bernie's answers were short and unusually strained, and he did little to extend the conversation. I think he was nervous around pretty ladies, and Mrs. Hostetler was certainly attractive. By the time we left her house, I think Bernie liked her almost as much as he did Sparkle Plenty.

After a couple more customers, we pushed away from South Main. It was time to tackle our Mount Everest for the day: Thatcherville Hill. This was not going to be easy, and I had mentally prepared Bernie and myself for the challenge. I figured at some point, probably about three-quarters of the way up, I'd need to pull Bernie's wheelchair instead of pushing it. He didn't seem to mind when I explained the procedure to him, but I also doubt he had ever been in the position of looking down a steep incline while being pulled up. Disaster was a possibility. If I slipped or lost my grip on the handles of his chair, he'd have the soapbox derby ride of his life without the soapbox, steering wheel, or brakes. I had to be super careful.

I had watched *Kiss of Death*, a 1940s gangster film noir, on television a few weeks before, and the wheelchair scene still haunted me. Richard Widmark plays the worst villain I'd ever seen, and he maniacally pushes an old lady in her wheelchair down a flight of stairs. I did not want to be remembered forever as the Rickie Widmark of DeGraff.

I had seven customers on the left going up Thatcherville, beginning with the Keenans and ending with Mr. and Mrs. Frantz, first-generation immigrants from Germany who owned a small vegetable market near the center of town. Eight customers were on the other side going down: Ethel Mooring at the top, down to Harry Nogle at the bottom. Usually I'd ride my bike fast and reckless down the rapid descent, but this day I needed to be slow and wreckless.

When Mrs. Keenan, the first stop before our thirty-three degree climb, saw me hauling Bernie, she had a conniption fit. A very protective and cautious lady with two kids of her own, she reacted as mothers are prone to do, seeing only the dangers of our adventure and not the benefits.

"Rickie, are you planning to roll him up Thatcherville?" she questioned, right arm pointing upward toward the hill.

"Yes, ma'am, I am, but I have a plan." Crap, I sounded like a kid, and I could tell by the look on her face she didn't think I had any plan at all.

"Does your mother know what you're doing?" Her matronly arms were now folded and locked tight.

"Yes, ma'am, she knows all about it. So does my dad." Even though Mrs. Keenan liked my parents, my confidence was draining fast. Bernie wasn't any help as he sat there, voiceless, counting pebbles in their driveway. The first time I'm in need of his support, and he becomes a pebble counter.

"If I called your mother right now, would she tell me she approves of this?"

Holy cow, Mrs. Keenan sounded like she did basic training under General George S. Patton!

"Yes, ma'am, she'd tell you it's okay with her."

Mrs. Keenan then unlocked her arms and in a surprisingly gentle voice said, "Then you be careful, very careful."

"Yes, ma'am, I will be very careful," I promised while wheeling Bernie toward the next house carefully, very carefully, like he was a crate of DeGraff Hatchery eggs.

The next four houses were uneventful. Two had envelopes hanging on the knob with my money inside, while Lula Taylor didn't even notice Bernie and old Mr. Painter just waved toward him. I'm not certain Mr. Painter even knew what he was waving at because he was pretty old with really thick glasses and could barely find his paper in the front bushes when I'd miss his porch.

After the Painter house, I pivoted Bernie's wheelchair to pull him up the rest of Thatcherville Hill. As I rotated him 180 degrees and had Bernie facing the downhill slope for the first time, I asked if he was okay. Bernie didn't answer, so I leaned forward to take a look at him. I had never seen his eyes so big—they were golf balls. Now he had doubts! But in the immortal words of Caesar, the die was cast, and we had nowhere to go but up. Neither of us said a word as we crept slowly up the hill step-by-step, roll-by-roll. I'll bet he never blinked his golf ball eyes until we reached Rita Thornton's house at the top and across the driveway from the Frantz house.

In all the time I'd known Bernie, I had never looked closely at his wheelchair until I began to tug it up the hill. The chair was solid and heavy with lots of chrome-plated metal, two inflated back tires, and smaller all-rubber wheels in front that swiveled for turning. Behind his back was a large, thickly folded towel that seemed attached to his chair, and he sat on a flat cushion extending side to side atop the stretched leather seat.

The wheelchair was Bernie's life and not a mere accessory to it, and I felt bad I hadn't given his chair the proper respect before our adventure. Now, when I see someone in a wheelchair, I consider the chair to be an extension of the person in it. I don't know if that's a good or bad thing, but I do it nonetheless.

The Thornton house was my final collection on the upside of Thatcherville Hill. The Frantzes were actually my last customers, but I collected from them at their vegetable market in town. Rita Thornton was the sexiest girl in my class, first through twelfth grade, and I felt blessed to have her on my route. Her full name was Rita Ann Thornton, and because of her initials, she was nicknamed Rat. But she was definitely no rodent and always Rita to me. She was extremely popular, a cheerleader, and on the homecoming court all four years of high school. Plus, she was a really nice girl.

When I was lucky, she'd be the one to pay me on Saturdays. As she talked nonstop about band or chorus—she played trumpet and sang soprano—I'd listen intently and fantasize. I think I was able to speed down Thatcherville Hill so quickly because, after a few minutes with Rita, my male hormone afterburners kicked in.

On this day I was her hero for bringing Bernie with me. "Oh my gosh, Rick, this is so cool. I can't believe you brought him all the way up. You really are a great guy."

Yeah, Rita, I thought to myself, if I'm such a great guy, why are you dating Butch Helmandollar and not me? Explain that one. But, since she'd brought out a box of gingersnap cookies, all was quickly forgiven.

Rita paid special attention to Bernie, and I admired her even more. For several months after our visit, Bernie asked about Rita, and I'd tell him she had asked about him as well. A few times she actually had. Guys like Bernie and me appreciated being asked about by girls like Rita. Male insecurities run deep at any age.

As we left Rita and crossed the street to begin our collection descent, something unusual was happening below. Down the hill and on each side of the road, people were standing on the sidewalks. Now, it wasn't exactly a crowd, and it certainly wasn't ceremonial, like college faculty in full academic regalia applauding graduating seniors. The gathering wasn't anything overly significant, although I wish I could remember it that way. But it was pretty special, especially for Bernie. I later found out that Mrs. Keenan had called her neighbors and asked them to be on the lookout for us, more for safety than for ceremony.

As we came down the hill, my customers stationed themselves at the front and back of Bernie's wheelchair to help me with him, walking up to the chair and greeting him by name. We took a while to finally reach Harry Nogle's house, the last customer on Thatcherville Hill, because everyone wanted to say something to Bernie. At Thatcherville's bottom we spent several extra minutes thanking everyone before saying our good-byes.

I pushed Bernie away and the hill flattened out into smooth road once again. We turned to look back. My customers were still outside laughing and talking with one another. "That's nice to see," I said aloud before turning Bernie around for the ride back to his house.

We were about twenty minutes away from Bernie's, and he talked most of the way back, reliving our adventure as he loved to do. I think Bernie met more people than he had in his entire life. The day had been an eventful one, and I could tell he was tired. He yawned several times, something I hadn't seen him do before.

Just before we reached his house, straight out of the blue Bernie blurted out, "She called you Rick."

"What'd you say? What are you talking about, Bernie?"

"Up at her house, Rita called you Rick."

"Yeah, so what? So what if she called me Rick?"

Bernie's reply was so earnest, I was caught completely off guard. "Do you want me to call you Rick?"

Bernie always surprised me. The way he processed things, thought about stuff, was way different than anyone I knew and certainly not the way I did. After several years of friendship, he was now concerned about what to call me. He was really something.

"No, Bernie," I assured him, "you can still call me Rickie. In fact I'd prefer it." At that time in my life I was Rick more often than I was Rickie, and being the typical kid who wanted to grow up quickly, I kind of liked the more adult-sounding Rick. But with Bernie, Rickie sounded natural.

"Good," he said, grinning his silly grin, "because Rick, my boy, doesn't sound so hot."

"No, Bernie, it doesn't."

"But Rickie, my boy, does." He rolled his eyes, pleased with himself. "Rickie, my boy, does."

I grabbed the sandwiches Mrs. Jones had made for us from behind the bushes, emptied the thermos, and sat it on the porch. It was after 1:00 p.m., and I was really running late, still having the last third of my route to collect as well as the afternoon papers to deliver.

I put my hand on Bernie's shoulder. "Great day, buddy, great day we had."

Looking sad and happy at the same time, his own sadappy, Bernie wobbled his head in agreement and repeated my words, "Great day, buddy, great day we had." I knew how he felt because our adventure had come to an end, and I was feeling a little down myself.

I pedaled away, scattering gravel right and left, and dropped the peanut butter sandwiches in a big trash bin by the box factory's main entrance.

The next day after lunch, Jeff and I were tossing a baseball back and forth in the front yard. Mr. Bethel, our across-the-street neighbor and school superintendent, an awkward combination for my family, walked to the edge of his driveway and called my name.

"Rick, I would like to talk to you for a couple of minutes."

"Sure, Mr. Bethel," I hollered while throwing the ball back to Jeff. Since I didn't know what he wanted, I held onto my glove like a security blanket just in case I was in some kind of trouble. As I jogged across the street toward Mr. Bethel, I could see he was smiling, so I figured I must not have done anything too bad.

"How are you doing today, Mr. Bethel?" I asked adult-like. "How was church?"

"I am very well, thank you, and our minister had a wonderful message. Let's have a seat around back. I want to talk to you."

We walked through the garage to the back patio where four redwood chairs were placed in orderly fashion around a redwood picnic table, a sweating pitcher of sun tea and two ice-filled glasses dominating the surface. I felt uncomfortable with my baseball glove still on my left hand and wished I had left it with Jeff. I removed the glove and quickly slid it under my chair.

Mr. Bethel filled our glasses with iced tea, and we sat for a moment without speaking. I gulped at my tea while he sipped his properly.

He broke the silence. "At church this morning, Mrs. Bethel and I heard about what you did for the Jones boy yesterday."

In DeGraff there were no secrets, and nothing out of the ordinary went unnoticed. Husbands dare not sneak around on their wives, and wives dare not wink at the delivery men.

"It really wasn't anything, Mr. Bethel. I just took Bernie around with me on part of my paper route. It really wasn't anything."

"Yes it was, Rick, yes it was. Your gesture was a very special one."

Adults always seem to read more than there is into a kid thing, sometimes for the better and sometimes for the worse. This was one of those over-read readings.

"Really, Mr. Bethel, it was nothing great. Bernie wanted to see part of my newspaper route, so I took him with me."

Mr. Bethel smiled the kind of smile adults do when they think they know more than you know but don't want to embarrass you.

"Rick, I want you to listen carefully to what I am about to say. No interruptions until I am finished. Will you agree?" I nodded. "I am going to ask a favor from you." He paused to take another sip of tea. "In a few years you will have a big decision to make, and as you are making it, I hope you will remember this request." He looked straight into my eyes as he spoke. "I want you to be a teacher. You have a kind heart, you care about people, and you do well in school. Those are the traits of an effective teacher, and I think you would be a fine one."

I really hadn't given much thought to what I wanted to be. Several years before I had told my Uncle Robert I wanted to be a professional whistler, but I hadn't improved my technique since then, so whistling for a living was probably out. Being a teacher hadn't entered my mind. Besides, I could never be as good a teacher as my dad, and comparisons to him would hound me from school to school my whole teacher life.

But I really did feel complimented by Mr. Bethel's words and his confidence in me. Except he was mostly wrong. I wasn't very kindhearted, and I only cared about certain people. But I was a good student, so he had a third of me right.

"Thank you, Mr. Bethel. I promise I'll consider it." And I think I really meant it, although I could not look him as straight in the eye as he had me.

He poured me another glass of tea, and leaning back comfortably in the chair, I sipped like a proper gentleman.

VI

Rules and Etiquette of Croquet

Not all of my encounters with Mr. Bethel were pleasant ones. From the very beginning, my dad was apprehensive about the Bethels living in our neighborhood and across the street from us. When Jack and Velma Boone moved out and Emery and Betty Bethel moved in, Dad became a nervous wreck. And for good reason. Mr. Bethel was the superintendent where Dad taught music and his boys attended school. The day the moving van arrived and the Bethels began to unpack was the day I heard my dad use a variation of the word "awkward" three times in the same sentence.

"No doubt about it. The awkwardness of this awkwardly situation is going to be unbelievably awkward!"

From his worrisome look and doomsday uttering, I gathered having the DeGraff school superintendent across the street was going to put a big dent in our uninhibited lives. I wasn't too concerned about me. No, I was worried about Jeff and Kurt. You never knew what they might do or say to embarrass the family and cause Dad to lose his job. At least those were my thoughts on the dilemma. I later learned that Dad hadn't singled out either of them, realizing any one of his sons or his wife or even he was capable of doing in the family. The school executive head was living across the street from us, and we were preparing for the worst. This could be awkward.

Without a doubt the Bethels added class to our neighborhood. It isn't as if we weren't a refined group already, but after watching them, we realized we were only small-town refined. Mr. Bethel remains one of few intellectuals who actually influenced my life, seeing potential in me that evaded other people's observations. However, even with my promising potential, life around Mr. Bethel was not always smooth.

The competitive nature of my family is well documented, and none of us gives an inch. Mom is as fiercely competitive as any among us but simply won't admit it. A pleasant Sunday afternoon game of croquet, two weeks after the Bethels moved in, gave Mr. Bethel his first indication of the Niece clan clamor.

Green is my favorite color, and I always used the green mallet and the green-striped ball for our croquet matches, but for some reason on that Sunday Jeff laid claim to them first. The blue ball and mallet were his usual choice, except when he was being contrary, and this was one of his contrary days. Dad was in no mood for our sibling squabbles, so Jeff was allowed to keep the green, and I was stuck with blue and an even bluer attitude.

I don't remember how it started, but suddenly and with great intensity, like a grease fire on the stove, the five of us were at one another, including Kurt, who was shorter than his mallet and just learning the game. One of us usually remained in control to serve as mediator, but not this time. Much like the United Nations if the translators decided to go on strike, we were all yelling at once with no one listening and not a word understandable anyway.

I was still blabbing indiscreetly for several seconds before I realized the rest of my family was in mute-button silence. I then noticed Mr. Bethel had slipped into our group. He shook his head in wonderment, handed my dad something, and left without a word. The mute button released, we noisily gathered around Dad to see what Mr. Bethel had delivered. In Dad's shaking hand was a small booklet entitled *Rules and Etiquette of Croquet*. We stared at it awkwardly.

Later that evening we had a study session to master the booklet, followed by a thorough review, and capped off with a quiz. Kurt was the only family member to pass.

The Bethel house was a relatively modest one before they moved in, with nothing distinctive to make it stand out from the rest of the Mill Street homes. But once they occupied it, the transformation was impressive: fresh paint, fancy shutters, new slate shingles, a resurfaced asphalt driveway, and artistic landscaping. The renovations occurred during the summer, and the process was amazing to watch. Once they finished, everything looked meticulous except for an out-of-control, fenced in, lantana-like half acre behind their perfectly preened backyard. The area was fondly known as the apple orchard, but the orchard hadn't seen a decent apple since Johnny Appleseed was a seedling—no upkeep, no produce.

Soon after the Bethels arrived, my mother proudly informed them that I was required to save four dollars a week from the paper route toward my college education. And I faithfully did. Every week of my paper delivering life, I dutifully saved four dollars toward my higher education. At the time I groused, grumbled, and pleaded for a never-once-awarded exemption. As I look back, my parental-imposed savings plan was the best lesson in financial discipline I ever received.

One day when I was in the front yard trying to teach Lady to count like Fern Burdette's Duke, Mr. Bethel walked over and asked if I wanted to earn some extra money. When the superintendent speaks, you pay attention, and I asked what he had in mind. He said he had heard about my college savings plan and guessed I could use a little extra spending money for myself. The man was perceptive.

"Tell you what," he proposed, "I will give you ten dollars to whip the apple orchard into shape and then five dollars every other week to keep it mowed and trimmed." My smile gave away my euphoria.

I kept my end of the agreement, and the apple orchard soon looked as presentable as the rest of the Bethel property. The first whacks at it took most of a prime summer weekend, but from then on the maintenance was like a biweekly trim in the barbershop.

One lazy afternoon before I was about to start mowing the orchard, Mrs. Bethel invited me into their house for a glass of iced tea. Carrying our teas on a silver tray, she led me into the den where Mr. Bethel was already seated. There I saw the reason I'd been invited in. Before me in all of its volumetric glory was the grandest high fidelity record playing system I'd ever seen. Mr. Bethel was understandably proud, and "His Master's Voice" had a most appreciative master.

"Are you familiar with Tchaikovsky's *1812 Overture*?" Mr. Bethel asked.

"I sure am," I replied, relieved he'd asked me about a classical piece I liked and not some obscure aria from an opera. I never wanted to bluff my way through anything with Mr. Bethel.

"Have you heard the overture the way Tchaikovsky wrote it to be played, with actual cannon shots instead of using timpani?"

"No, sir," I said, now in awe, "actual cannon shots?"

"Yes, the *1812 Overture* was written to commemorate Napoleon's failed attempt to overthrow the Russian Empire. Tchaikovsky used the salvos of cannon shots to represent Russia's successful resistance."

I already knew the story behind the overture, but Mr. Bethel sounded so professorial I felt like I was hearing it for the first time. He lifted the diamond-needled arm, gently placed it on the record, and Mr. Tchaikovsky's wondrous work filled the room. In our house the only source for classical music was a compact, gray vinyl-covered Silvertone Tru-Phonic Phonograph that scratched out nearly recognizable monophonic sounds from Dad's collection of classical recordings. But the Silvertone's tiny speakers were no match for Mr. Bethel's golden-toned ones. I have never been more mesmerized, and for seventeen glorious minutes I was in a concert hall with Peter Ilyich Tchaikovsky and the London Philharmonic.

About three quarters through the overture, I knew the cannon blasts were mere measures away. The first cannon rattled the ice cubes in my tea, and they kept rattling at every blast. As the long final crescendo began and the victory bells chimed in, I prepared myself for the second series of cannon shots by loosely holding my tabled glass to feel the vibrations. The cannons echoed through me. And then silence. After a respectful pause, Mr. Bethel asked what I thought. He could tell by the loss-for-words expression on my face that I was unable to explain the beauty of what I had just experienced.

"I understand." He nodded. "The music leaves me speechless as well. You can replay it in your head, again and again, as you mow the orchard."

And I did replay it—each note, each measure, each cannon shot. Fantasizing about a career as the first chair whistler for the London Phil-harmonic, I mowed the last swatch just as I whistled my full crescendo big finish. Uncle Robert would have been proud.

VII

Among the Entrepreneurs

All small towns have their gathering places for social gossip and friendly chatter. One of DeGraff's popular spots was Taylor's Restaurant, run by Wig and Becky Taylor. Near the center of downtown and across the street from the DeGraff Public Library, the restaurant did a brisk business with hometown regulars throughout the day. Becky was a superb cook, especially her hamburgers, and Wig was an exemplary host/waiter/cashier/busboy/host. The two of them ran the whole show with occasional assistance from daughter Cat.

Cold and wintry Saturdays were my favorite times to stop at Taylor's Restaurant. Halfway through collecting for the weekly paper, I'd hurry in to warm up with a steaming cup of Becky's hot chocolate. Thankfully, packets of instant hot chocolate hadn't reached rural Ohio.

Becky made her hot chocolate from scratch, magically mixing milk, cream, sugar, butter, and thick-barred semi-sweet chocolate in an iron pan on the stove and coaxing the dark brown ambrosia to a perfect simmer. She'd then carefully ladle her elixir into marshmallow-laded, wide-brim mugs for Wig to serve awaiting customers. Cold and wintry Saturday breaks at Taylor's Restaurant were special times.

One extremely cold, double-digit below zero Saturday morning, I clumped into Taylor's numbed and icicled. I had imagined Becky's hot chocolate since my first steps outside, and the enkindling vision kept me from freezing stiff. Wig greeted me at the counter with grim reaper news.

"No hot chocolate today, Rickie. Becky's down with the flu and Cat's cooking, but she won't consider attempting her mother's hot chocolate. How about a cup of my java?"

I hadn't been that disappointed since the Christmas I'd been expecting a puppy, but Mom and Dad brought home my baby brother Jeff instead. Coffee instead of hot chocolate! How about liver instead of lasagna? Brussels sprouts instead of brownies? Ragweed instead of roses? Ma Kettle instead of Annette Funicello? I'd only had one drink of coffee in my life, and that singular sip was more than enough to last a lifetime. I could not imagine consuming an entire cup of the stuff. Coffee instead of hot chocolate, no way!

But my brain was frozen. "Sure," I answered, cold and desperate. "Sure, pour me a cup."

I don't know if it was the disappointment of not having Becky's hot chocolate or if it was simply that Wig Taylor didn't know beans about making a decent cup of java. I don't know what it was. But that swallow ruined coffee and me. I haven't tasted another drop since. I don't even like Kahlúa.

DeGraff's prominent leaders were frequent visitors to Taylor's, and many business deals, both consequential and insignificant, were conceived and born there. I enjoyed sipping my hot chocolate at the counter while watching the impressive paper shuffling going on in one of the corner booths. Fantasizing about the economic windfalls my small town would soon reap from these big transactions, I was honored to be a mere paperboy seated among the cavalcade of entrepreneurs.

A few years before my newspaper delivering days, I'd had my first experience with an entrepreneur, my Granddad Niece. He and my grandmother owned a small clothing store in another town several miles from DeGraff.

When I was five, I loved pre-newspaper Saturdays because that was the day my dad and I traveled to their rustic boutique, The Urban Store. Through the eyes of a little boy, the store seemed like a gigantic, big city Macy's. In reality it was merely a small, family-run, mom and pop all-purpose clothing store.

My dad assisted with taking the inventory on Saturdays, and I'd be left to walk in wonderment through the mystical maze of aisles and narrow passageways that racks of clothing magically make. The store was a textiled farmland of fascination, a garmented field sown with row after row of multicolored fabric, texture, and design all ripe and ready for the shoppers' harvest.

For some reason even little boys cannot explain, I was mesmerized by the solitary shoe display dominating a well-lit corner at the back of the store. The shoes were a collage of styles, shapes, sizes, and shades, and each Saturday the shoes displayed seemed to be different than those from the week before, except for one pair. I noticed that the same pair of dark brown men's shoes sat in the same spot Saturday after Saturday. I was puzzled because all of the other shoes disappeared quickly.

One Saturday when the dusty shoes had been in their identical positions for several weeks, I decided to examine them. I had no idea what I was looking for when I cautiously reached out for the right shoe with both hands. After I lifted the shoe, its dusty outline remained on the display shelf, and I realized, in my slow-to-comprehend little boy reasoning, that these shoes had not been moved for a long time. Cradling the shoe like some sort of ancient Egyptian artifact, I ran to the front of the store to find my grandfather and share this amazing discovery with him.

My grandfather was in his office shifting through stacks of bills and receipts when I excitedly rushed up to him and asked why this shoe and its mate had remained on the shelf for so long. He smiled at me and gently removed the shoe from my embrace, while motioning me to sit beside him in his leather desk chair. I was always fascinated by his office and excited to join him there. A picture of a man in a cowboy hat hung on the wall above his massive roll-top desk, and the first time I asked who the man was, he told me that was his idol, Will Rogers. I asked if Will Rogers could be my idol, too, and he generously said we could share him.

As we sat behind the desk, he shared his secret about the shoe. While rotating it slowly, he explained he'd never cared for the shoes, but a regional salesman from Florscheims talked him into buying them, convincing him the shoes were the newest fashion rage and podiatric statement in men's footwear. The salesman obviously did not know fashion trends in rural Ohio. Against his better entrepreneurial instincts, my grandfather bought the pair.

He then squeezed my shoulder and shared an insight I haven't forgotten. He said he continued to leave the shoes on display as a reminder to never again try to sell something he didn't believe in himself. Those were powerful words for a little boy to understand, but I grasped his lesson.

My grandfather and I walked back to the display and carefully replaced the shoe within the dusty pattern beside its companion. The shoes remained unsold until his death and the store's eventual closing. Will Rogers never met a man he didn't like, and he'd have especially liked my grandfather, the first real entrepreneur in my life.

So I felt at ease on Saturdays, sipping Becky Taylor's rich hot chocolate while sharing a work break with DeGraff's entrepreneurs. Although we didn't exactly rub shoulders, we did drink from the same mugs.

Gil Mooring, president and principal owner of the People's Building & Loan, was a no-nonsense businessman and restaurant regular. His mother was a customer on my paper route, and through the two of them I was about to learn another unforgettable lesson.

DeGraff was a rural area surrounded by dozens of small, family-owned farms. Farming was a constant struggle for the hard-working families held hostage by Ohio's fickle weather, and many farmers needed second and third mortgages to stay afloat. Gil Mooring was their ready savior and quickly became the major lender in town, gaining the trust of the farming community.

Gil's mother, Ethel Mooring, lived at the top of the west side of Thatcherville Hill. Her home was the newest one in the neighborhood, all brick with white shuttered windows, and Gil had it built for her after his father's death. Although a delightful and engaging lady, Mrs. Mooring had none of her son's financial sense. Collecting from her was always a challenge as she'd insist on under- or overpaying me. She'd remember when the paper was a dime for the week or she'd think it was fifty cents, with never much common ground in between. One Saturday Gil was visiting his mother as I was attempting to collect, and he quickly got the picture. After Mrs. Mooring and I settled on thirty cents for the fourth time, he walked me to my bicycle.

Hands in his pocket and posed like he was addressing a business colleague, he laid out a plan. "Tell you what. Why don't you just stop by my office each week, and I will pay you for Mother's paper. That should save you the frustration and her the time. Agreed?"

I liked his idea immediately and thought it would work. But it didn't work, and very soon an even bigger problem developed. Gil Mooring was seldom available when I stopped in the People's Building & Loan to collect, usually out of his office or in with a client. I guess I was no longer his business colleague because when I told the secretary I was his newspaper proprietor and needed to see him on personal business, she didn't even suggest an appointment. Instead, she smiled and handed me a lollipop.

After several weeks, the bill reached serious proportions: the Moorings owed me $2.10. The plan was a disaster, and part of my weekly profit was somewhere in Gil Mooring's pocket.

One afternoon when I was delivering the newspapers, I saw Gil Mooring leave Taylor's Restaurant. I did a quick U-turn and pedaled up to him. "Mr. Mooring, I'd like to collect for the paper," I said innocently, or at least I thought it was innocent. I was about to learn a lesson.

Gil Mooring was incensed, and he took a full minute to compose himself. After a deep breath, he started to lecture me. "Listen to me, young man, and listen very carefully." He paused deliberately. "A gentleman never asks another gentleman for money on the street. Business transactions are not conducted in that manner. A gentleman always requests money in private. Financial dealings are personal matters." He stopped, peering down and searching my face for a reaction. "Do you understand?" At the moment I had only one thought: Will Rogers never met Gil Mooring.

"Yes, Mr. Mooring, I understand, and I'm sorry I asked you in public for the money you owe me. I won't do it again, sir." My parents taught me to respect my elders.

"Good, then we have an understanding," he said, turning toward the People's Building & Loan. "Now, I have an appointment, and a businessman is never late for an appointment." With that, he was gone.

Actually, I learned two important lessons that day from Gil Mooring, president and principle owner of People's Building & Loan. First, never publicly ask a gentleman for money. Second, never be late for an appointment. But no matter how invaluable his lessons were, I was still out $2.10. Now, however, I had my own lesson to teach, and I was enrolling as the first pupil: Get 'em while you got 'em or they're gonna be gone!

The next week I made an official appointment through Mr. Mooring's secretary. I was persistent in making the appointment and twice refused her offer of a cherry lollipop. After he paid me the new and astronomical total of $2.40, we agreed to another plan. He'd leave the money for his mother's paper with his secretary, and I'd collect from her. The plan worked, and I looked forward each week to guessing what flavor lollipop I'd be offered.

A couple of months later, as I was nursing a hot chocolate in the back corner booth and carefully reviewing my ledger of customer collections, Gil Mooring strolled into Taylor's Restaurant, sat at the counter, and ordered a cup of coffee. When I paid Wig for my hot chocolate, I included a dime for Gil Mooring's coffee. As I opened the door to leave, I gave him a tip of my baseball cap, and he smiled. I think he was impressed. I know Will would have been.

VIII

Trick or Treat with *The Daily Planet*

I felt lucky to be a paperboy. The pay was steady at ten cents a week per customer, and with seventy-two customers that was a cool $7.20. Four dollars of my weekly profit was put toward college, but the remaining $3.20 went a long way in DeGraff's modest cost of living economy. I didn't exactly live high on the hog—with twenty-five-cent movie tickets, ten-cent comic books, and nickel RC Colas and candy bars being among my extravagances—but I was almost up to the pig rib cage.

As a paperboy, I also enjoyed aristocratic privileges beyond the financial ones because my customers kept me well fed. Cookies, pies, cakes, brownies, and apple dumplings were culinary perks, but my favorite among the favored treats was Miss Lizzie Moore's pumpkin bread. She baked petite, brick-sized loaves to golden brown perfection and dressed each one individually in a creaseless coat of aluminum foil. On holidays only Miss Lizzie seemed to celebrate, like Groundhog Day, Arbor Day, and Armistice Day ending World War I, she would offer me a foiled loaf along with my weekly payment for the newspaper through her slightly opened screen door. Miss Lizzie celebrated holidays the rest of us forgot while never seeming to remember the notable ones.

Miss Lizzie was a curiosity of legendary status in DeGraff, and her legend was a sad one. Few citizens remembered seeing her in public. My only not-through-the-screen-door glimpse of her had been the Saturday

Bernie and I collected for the paper, when she stepped beyond the door of her small world and into the outside universe of ours. The reclusive Miss Lizzie was DeGraff's Emily Dickinson.

According to Sam Hamsher, our unofficial resident historian who knew a little bit of something about everyone in DeGraff, Miss Lizzie once worked in a mail sorting car of the New York Central Railroad. The train used to pass daily on the tracks by Bernie's house and the box factory, long before either was constructed. Miss Lizzie sorted mail with a man named Dewey Daniel Stanton, nicknamed Dewstan by his paternal grandfather.

As often happens when two people work within close proximity, they became friendly, courted, and fell in love. One late October afternoon the train made its usual stop for coal and water at the DeGraff Depot, a structure razed three decades later to make way for the box factory. In a quiet corner of the Depot, Dewstan asked Miss Lizzie to marry him. She accepted, and they planned a June wedding for the following summer: the summer of 1917.

Fate indifferently meddled in their plans, as fate often does, and the United States entered World War I on April 6, 1917. The wedding was postponed because Dewstan enlisted in the Army and was shipped overseas. The following year Dewey Daniel Stanton died in France as he and his doughboy comrades defended the Marne River Line at Chateau-Thierry.

Miss Lizzie quit her mailroom job for the NYC Railroad and built a small house near the Depot where Dewstan had proposed. And there she lived to old age, receiving *The Bellefontaine Examiner* six days a week, seldom venturing beyond her front door, and becoming a curiosity of legendary status in DeGraff.

I liked Miss Lizzie and respected her solitude, and in time she began to like me. After we'd have a conversation, always shared through her screen door, I'd be rewarded the following day with a loaf of flawlessly foiled pumpkin bread. I'd also receive a loaf on those special holidays only Miss Lizzie remembered to celebrate.

During my junior year in high school and the week before Halloween, Miss Lizzie made a startling request when I stopped to collect for the paper. Her request was a doozy. She asked if Bernie and I could help her give out treats to the trick-or-treaters. This fragile, cloistered whisper of a lady who barely opened her door to me when I collected for the paper was going to celebrate Halloween by encouraging pint-sized goblins, pirates, and witches to knock on her door. I cannot imagine the look on my face when she asked me to assist.

I finally managed to stammer, "What are you going to give them, Miss Lizzie?"

She looked as stunned at my question as I had at her request. "Why, young man, it's Halloween. I think pumpkin bread is the perfect treat for Halloween, don't you?" Who was I to question the obvious?

I could not wait to tell Bernie. Bernie lived for out-of-the-ordinary stuff, and celebrating Halloween with Miss Lizzie was certainly bound to crack into the top ten out-of-the-ordinary events on his fantasy list of potential adventures. After I told him about Miss Lizzie, Bernie caught me off guard with his question. That was not my day to predict the predictable.

"But, Rickie, my boy, what are we going to be?"

My vacant, furrowed-brow look answered for me, so Bernie repeated himself with unmistakable clarity. "What are we going to wear? Who are we going to dress up like?"

Costumes! I hadn't even considered costumes. Before I could give his question any creative thought, he answered for both of us.

"I've got it! I'll be Superman, and you'll be Clark Kent."

Superman was Bernie's second favorite hero, next in line to Dick Tracy. He'd been a fan of the television program, *The Adventures of Superman*, for several years and was still disappointed at its cancellation. The program's simplistic plots revolved around Superman's heroics in Metropolis, the newspaper offices of *The Daily Planet*, and the inept but lovable reporters Clark Kent, Lois Lane, and Jimmy Olson. I think Bernie had a crush on Lois Lane, but I could never get him to admit it.

"Bernie," I tried my best to reason with him, "Clark Kent and Superman are the same person. You and I do not look enough alike for you to be Superman and me Clark Kent. Besides, the two of them couldn't be in a room together because they were the same guy. They were the same guy, Bernie. How are you and I going to pass out treats together in the same room as the same guy?"

He gave me an icy stare with his controlled eyes, and I felt like he had caught me selling imported Kryptonite to gangsters. My reasoned logic seldom held a ghost of a chance against Bernie's illogical logic, and I had learned over the years when not to argue with him. After he'd made up his mind about something, there was no unmaking it, and this was a no-unmaking situation.

"Okay, Bernie, you be Superman, and I'll be Clark Kent. But what about Miss Lizzie?"

I knew I had him.

He paused a Bernie pause, one of those rare instances when his eyes would unfocus and roam beyond me. After he gathered his thoughts, he began flapping his arms and legs in absolute non-precision. "She'll be Lois Lane! We'll stick a pencil behind her ear and give her a notebook."

And that was that. This Halloween was going to be trick or treat with *The Daily Planet.*

As I delivered the paper each day leading up to Halloween, Miss Lizzie greeted me from behind the screen door and beckoned me toward her with an enticing invitation. "Try this batch of pumpkin bread, hot from the oven."

After jabbing her arm around the screen door to hand me a slice, freshly buttered and snuggled on a napkin, she'd study me with her head cocked slightly to the right and not breathing until I chewed and swallowed. I'd quickly brag, "Miss Lizzie, this is delicious. It may be the best one yet."

And it may have been. In all the years I sampled her pumpkin bread, I honestly never knew if one loaf was better than another. They were all superb month after month, year after year. As a baker, Miss Lizzie was consistently consistent. The day before Halloween, after serving as official taste tester during the week before our grand giveaway, I asked the question that had been nagging at me.

"Miss Lizzie, how many loaves are you baking?"

She winked. "Just enough, I'm certain, just enough."

I had no idea how to quantify "just enough" and doubted she did either.

As I delivered Bernie's paper on the day of our big night, he was in full excitement overload and not the least bit interested in *Dick Tracy*. For that day Dick was on his own pursuing bad guys. "What time you coming back, Rickie, my boy?"

DeGraff's traditional time for kids and their parents to trick or treat was 7:00 p.m. to 8:30 p.m. I figured I needed at least an hour before the costumed arrivals to push Bernie to Miss Lizzie's and help prepare for the onslaught of little beggars.

"Bernie, I'll be back around six. Is your Superman costume ready?"

He cast a sideways, sheepish-eyed glance fairly close to my direction. "Yeah, I guess."

Any lack of excitement, especially on a night like this, wasn't Bernie-like, and his subdued mood was way out of character.

"What do you mean, you guess?"

"You'll see, Rickie, you'll see."

When I returned an hour later to wheel him to Miss Lizzie's, I saw the source of his concern. My Clark Kent disguise was extremely minimal, consisting only of a pair of my dad's oversized, outdated horn-rimmed glasses with the lenses removed. Miss Lizzie's Lois Lane was extremely practical with a yellow, freshly sharpened number two pencil to cradle behind her ear and a Hytone spiral notebook to tuck into her apron.

And Bernie? Well, Bernie as Superman was a combination of minimal, practical, and outright comically embarrassing. Superman Bernie, DeGraff's superhero for the evening, wore a cape consisting of his dad's red flannel long johns tied by the sleeves around his neck, the buttoned trapdoor and legs dangling over the back of his chair.

Unsuccessfully stifling my laughter, I tried my best to convince Bernie he looked superhero worthy. He didn't buy it and let me know how he felt about my disingenuousness with a sarcastic, "Yeah, right!"

And he was right. Sitting there with his face as ruby red as the underwear wrapped around his neck, Bernie looked pretty silly. In fact the three of us looked silly. But on that Halloween night, my favorite Halloween of all time, it didn't matter.

I pushed Bernie to Miss Lizzie's and onto the front porch. The screen door and front door were propped open, allowing me to roll Bernie into Miss Lizzie's secret world.

The interior was neat and well kept. Everything looked comfortably in place except for the dining room table that had been moved close to the front door, lines of table leg tracks still visible on the carpet from being dragged across it. My eyes followed the tracks to a small bay window and four dimples in the carpet where the table's feet had obviously rested for a long time before their short journey.

The table was now serving a new purpose, one I doubt it had ever served before. Assembled on its linen-laced top was a perfectly triangle-shaped stack of foil-covered pumpkin loaves—a pharaoh's pyramid of silver bricks mounded as carefully as the gold bars shelved in Fort Knox and every bit as precious. I mentally tried to count them but kept losing track.

"Miss Lizzie, how many loaves did you bake?"

Again she answered non-quantifiably, "Enough."

As she smiled while looking at the piled high table, then back to Bernie and me, I carefully examined, as I had never done before, the face framing her smile. I'd seen her face hundreds of times through the screen door and once in the sunlight on the porch, but I hadn't looked closely at Miss Lizzie until now. Her delicately cast face reminded me of the countenance on a cameo brooch my father bought in Naples for my mother during WWII: warmly pink and finely detailed. I saw, even after all these years later, how Dewey Daniel Stanton had fallen in love with this visage of solitude.

Bernie broke into my impolite inspection with an urgent insistence. "Rickie, my boy, give Miss Lizzie her costume!"

I handed Miss Lizzie the pencil and spiral notebook I'd been cradling under my arm since we entered her house. She was amused and cooperative while having no earthly idea who Lois Lane was. I doubt she'd even heard of Superman and assumed, looking at Bernie, he was simply a man in a wheelchair who wore long underwear around his neck.

We still had half an hour before show time, so Miss Lizzie expertly dissected a freshly baked pumpkin loaf into four fat slabs and thickly lathered each one with butter. A pitcher of milk shared the tarnished tray with three large mugs, and I poured the milk for us and helped Bernie with his portions. Miss Lizzie nibbled at her bread politely while Bernie and I devoured ours like we had missed supper.

While chomping my second slice, I noticed a small cherrywood table in the back corner of the living room. A metal table lamp with tassel-like fringe around the rose-colored shade illuminated several symmetrically placed items stationed beneath it. I walked over to look closer.

The table was actually an old-fashioned writing desk with a built-in inkwell and worn quill pen centered at the top. Three military medals and a faded red, white, and blue ribbon surrounded and captured the black-and-white picture of a solemn-faced doughboy. Her Bible was opened to Psalms with a yellow Western Union telegram sliced between the pages, pages now parchment-like from not being turned for years. Beside the Bible in a neatly yarn-wrapped collection were several letters, the top one with a French postmark and stamp. I tilted my head trying to read the address.

"I never opened the last of his letters." Miss Lizzie then paused before explaining what was none of my business. "As long as they remain unopened, I do not have to respond."

She folded her hands in her lap, and nothing more was said. I returned to my chair, and the three of us sat in silence waiting for our visitors. The time passed, and I fed Bernie the rest of his pumpkin bread, feeling more at ease than awkward with the quiet. Then, a tiny knock at the door, followed by a series of little knuckle knockings brought us back to Halloween. They were here.

Once the masquerade parade began, it continued seamlessly. And what a parade it was! We assembly lined our giveaway process and filled the bags' eagerly opened mouths so efficiently that Henry Ford would have been proud. Except our "tin Lizzies" were a different model than his and crafted by a single set of hands. Miss Lizzie guided the loaves onto Bernie's waiting lap, while I rhythmically lifted two at a time and set them gently into waiting, half-filled sacks.

Word about the generous treats at Miss Lizzie's must have spread town-wide because, I will swear, every DeGraff household was eventually at her door. Childless adults were borrowing their neighbors' kids to lead them to our bounty. Kids as shills were a rarity in DeGraff, but this night shilling was forgiven. I even saw two station wagons filled with kids from Quincy, the neighboring town.

No one noticed our costumes, or at least no one mentioned them, until the evening was almost over. As I was placing a shiny loaf into the bag of a little princess, she looked inside the house and saw Bernie.

"Daddy, look! It's Superman!" Her father peeked inside, smiled, and shook his head, looking equally amazed and bewildered. It didn't matter. That one moment of affirmation was all Bernie needed. I patted him on the shoulder and straightened his flowing cape over the wheelchair.

Amazingly, the very last knock of the evening received the very last pumpkin loaf. Miss Lizzie's "enough," like my Grandma Ruth's pinch of salt and sprinkle of sugar, was exactly right.

We sat for a few minutes smugly proud and reminiscing about our busy evening, while debating which children were the most creatively dressed. Bernie was unusually quiet, and knowing him as I did, I understood the reason. The end of something anxiously anticipated was difficult for him because daily routine was waiting next in his long line of ordinary.

As we were about to say our good nights, Miss Lizzie went into the kitchen and returned with two neatly folded Fuson's IGA grocery bags. She handed me one and placed the other on Bernie's lap.

"I'll bet you thought I had forgotten you. Trick or treat!"

I opened my bag, and nested inside were four foiled loaves tied together by a ribbon and handmade bow.

Miss Lizzie leaned down and kissed Bernie on the cheek. "Bless you, Bernie, bless you." She opened the front door and held the screen door wide for me to wheel him through, and as I did, she put her arm around my waist and pulled herself close. I felt the rhythm of her heart through her ever-tightening grasp.

"Thank you for a wonderful week, my friend."

I turned to kiss her forehead, but before I could reach her, she had moved away and was already screened behind the door.

"Good night, Miss Lizzie. Thanks for the pumpkin bread," was all I could manage before the front door closed tightly.

Bernie and I didn't speak as I wheeled him toward his house. When we reached the porch, the light came on, and Bernie's mother opened the door. She took the chair's handles from my hands and maneuvered him inside.

As I was walking away, Bernie called out, "Rickie, that little girl, she knew I was Superman!"

I turned toward him. "Yes she did, Bernie, yes she did. Your costume was perfect, buddy, the best of the evening. Good night."

The Halloween moon was not quite full, but the light was bright enough to distort my vision and distend the shadows to twice their size. I came to the railroad tracks and quickened my pace to cross them, but in mid-track I heard the blast of a train whistle. That was strange because no trains passed through DeGraff at that time of night. I froze and looked down the tracks in the direction of the sound. Just beyond the shadows' reach, I saw the pale figure of a man in uniform facing me. The whistle blew again, this time sounding even closer, and the penumbral silhouette drifted backward, legs not moving, into the enfolding shadows.

I blinked twice to refocus my eyes, trying to recapture the image and disbelieve the unbelievable. I couldn't.

Clutching the bag and my dad's lensless glasses, I jumped over the rest of the tracks and sprinted all the way home, looking back only once.

LETTERS

I enjoy rereading
        letters from
        Pliny the Younger,
        the Apostle Paul,
        Robert Browning and Elizabeth Barrett,
        Mark Twain,
        Martin Luther King,
        and my great-great-grandparents.
I am not embarrassed about
        being a benign interloper,
        curious and distant,
        officious yet respectful.
Letters
        become public readings
            of private lives
                as primary sources.
Letters
        sent to generations
        in their time,
        now for generations
        through time,
        correspond to me.
Letters of
        love
            hope
                passion
        peace
            fear
                remorse.

Letters,
　　　the bookmarks
　　　　　of times past
　　　revived again by us
　　　　　who snoop.
Even letters
　　　never opened
　　　never read
leave a message
mystically strong and painful.
What letters
　　　will this generation
　　　　　leave as a legacy?
Who will carefully
　　　yarn wrap and double bow
text messages?

IX

The Great Hamburger-Eating Contest

Taylor's Restaurant was the only place in DeGraff to buy a home-style meal. No one dared to open a competing eatery for fear it would die a painfully slow death of patronless starvation. In those days some monopolies were good. Our family seldom ate a meal that wasn't mom-prepared and in our kitchen, but when we did, Taylor's Restaurant was the treat of treats. I looked forward to my Saturday newspaper collections, especially the point midway through the route when a mug of Becky Taylor's homemade hot chocolate, richer than Hershey, Pennsylvania, awaited me.

In addition to hot chocolate, Becky also grilled amazing hamburgers long before Dave "Wendy's" Thomas from Columbus, Ohio, conceived his brilliantly bunned beef patties. My guess is Dave was passing through DeGraff one pleasant day, decided to stop by Taylor's Restaurant for a hamburger lunch, and presto grease-o, his successful franchise was conceived. That's how good Becky Taylor's hamburgers were.

Wimpy Knight was a restaurant regular who also drove the school bus for DeGraff's rural routes. Wimpy was a hefty giant of a man who everybody liked, especially kids. His bus route covered the fringe areas of DeGraff and included the farm families. Sometimes when I'd spend the weekend at Ned Heintz's farm, I'd get to ride Wimpy's bus to school with Ned on Monday morning, and that was a fun adventure for a city boy.

I suppose Wimpy had a real name, but I never heard it. Sam Hamsher dubbed him Wimpy after watching him eat two dozen White Castle hamburgers in a single sitting. Although White Castle hamburgers are junior sized, the accomplishment was an impressive feat. From that day on he was known as Wimpy, sharing the name with Popeye's hamburger-inhaling friend.

DeGraff was also home to Howard "Turkey" Thompson, nicknamed Turkey by his mother after Howard ate an entire twenty-pound turkey the Thanksgiving of his eighth grade year. According to town lore, Turkey's mother was button-popping proud of her boy's appetite and the new handle she gave him, although the other family members were miffed after seeing their plates stacked low with Fuson's IGA ham loaf.

One fall Friday night after a home football game, Dad chauffeured all of us to Taylor's Restaurant for a post-game meal. As we squeezed into a front booth and began to scan the menu, I noticed Wimpy seated at the busy counter with a plate of hamburgers in front of him. He hadn't started to eat and appeared to be ogling the herd for his first wrangle.

At that moment Turkey Thompson, now a tenth grader, loudly entered the restaurant. Turkey spied Wimpy's mounded platter of burgers and trumpeted, "Hey, Wimpy, is that all you can eat? What's the deal, are you on a diet?" He bellowed a hearty fat-guy laugh. "I guess you are wimpy!" He bellowed again as only tenth grade, amply girthed boys are apt to do. "I eat more than that for a pre-snack snack. In fact, Mr. Hamburger Man, I'll bet I can eat more hamburgers than you." Turkey's bantering had everyone's attention. The taunt was tossed, the challenge cast, the dare delivered, and the grease was eyeing the grill.

Before Wimpy could respond, Wig Taylor jumped in with a profitable proposal. "Tell you what, boys. Becky will cook all the hamburgers either one of you can eat. Whoever eats the most will be declared the winner. The deal is the loser pays for all hamburgers. What do you think? Do we have a contest?" Wig was a crafty one.

Without hesitation Wimpy and Turkey shook meat hooks, and Becky peppered the grill with a slew of raw patties. Wig removed the plate sitting patiently in front of Wimpy and announced he wanted each contestant to have a fresh start. All of the customers, including my family with Jeff lofted on Dad's shoulders and Mom cradling Kurt, began to crowd the counter to seek a better view. The Great Hamburger-Eating Contest was about to commence in Taylor's Restaurant.

But just before Becky finished the first batch of burgers, a noise squeaked from behind the crowd in the familiar high-pitched voice of Frank Tully. Now, Frank Tully was an oddity of indefinable proportions. He looked like the character actor Joe Besser, a replacement Stooge toward the end of the Three Stooges' heyday and the bratty "Stinky" of *Abbott and Costello* fame. DeGraff's Frank Tully looked more like Joe Besser than Stinky did.

No one knew for certain what Frank did for a living. The rumor was that his mother, who he'd lived with all of his life, had inherited wealth and, after her death, Frank inherited it. But that was only a rumor. No one knew for certain, not even Sam Hamsher.

What was known for certain was that Frank Tully never missed a civic event, a school event, a sports event, a church event, or even an insignificant event. Frank Tully defined ubiquitous. He was everywhere for everything within walking distance. I just assumed attendance was his occupation, like my dad's occupation was being a music teacher. An interview with Frank Tully by a *Bellefontaine Examiner* reporter would have gone something like this.

"What do you do for a living, Mr. Tully?" Stretching to his full 5'2" height with bald head sparkling, Frank Tully responds, "I attend, sir. I am an attendee, a professional attendee. I am in attendance."

So it was not unusual for Frank Tully to be somewhere among the crowd of people at Taylor's Restaurant that evening. What was unusual was for him to venture forth in such a bold manner. His helium-filled voice hovered above the crowd like a funny paper's cartoon caption before expanding, popping, and spilling words over us all.

"Mr. Taylor, can I eat hamburgers too? Can I be in this contest?" Frank's words were met with absolute silence, and the only sound was the sizzling of Becky's patties ganging on the grill. Bud Amos broke the spell.

"Let him in, Wig. Old Frank ain't gonna hurt nothin'. He's just a squirt."

Laughter exploded as everyone looked to Wig for his answer.

"It's all right with me if it's okay with Wimpy and Turkey. What do you say, boys?"

Wimpy smiled. "Sure."

"Fine by me," Turkey said with a smirk.

"Agreed then," Wig declared. "The two losers foot the bill."

The crowd split so Frank could scamper through to the counter. Turkey flabbed over to the next stool, and Frank squeezed in between him and Wimpy. Looking at the three of them was a sight to behold, especially from behind the behinds. Wimpy and Turkey's big butts engulfed the counter stools like suction cups, while Frank's modest one perched him atop his stool like a toad wedged between two farm pond bullfrogs. The gluttonous trio of Turkey, Wimpy, and Shrimpy looked ready to sing for their suppers.

By now Becky had prepared several well-stacked layers of hamburgers, and Wig slapped three burgers on each of three plates and slid them in front of the two gifted gastronomes and Frank. To wash the food down, Wimpy requested bottles of Coke, and Turkey demanded Dr. Pepper. Frank, the amateur of the three, simply wanted water. And with that the contest was on.

Since it was a challenge of consumption and not speed, each one ate in his own unique style. Wimpy chomped around the hamburger circle-like, then popped the core into his mouth while reaching for the next one. Turkey ate greedily and ravenously, eyes shifting rapidly side-to-side like he was checking to be certain his food was safe from predators. Since Turkey Thompson came from a big family of big people of big eaters of big portions, his suspicious nature came naturally.

Frank was his usual odd wonderment. He ate his hamburgers like New England blue bloods nibble their watercress finger sandwiches during afternoon high tea—deliberately, daintily, and dependably. Dependably was the key descriptor. Frank was dependability squared and squared again.

Turkey began to fade after his third plate of three burgers and folded altogether during the fourth. He had underestimated the size of Becky's hamburgers. Suctioning off the stool, then tottering toward the front door with both hands clasped to mouth, he gargled a good-bye and was not seen again for three weeks. Turkey later swore he didn't eat another hamburger until his junior year at Ohio State.

Wimpy looked strong until the seventh plate was set before him, while still having one hamburger left on the sixth. He surveyed the plate, glanced over toward Frank who was chewing dependably on his eighth hamburger, and stared back at his own plate. He then set the full plate in front of Frank.

"I'm stopping at seventeen, my little friend. Now I'm going to watch you bust trying to better that."

The remainder of The Great Hamburger-Eating Contest is committed to DeGraff folklore. It was almost 11:00 p.m., and the massive crowd had already thinned out. Dad said it was well past our bedtimes, and none of us argued with him. Jeff and Kurt had been sleeping for the past hour, Jeff in one of the booths and Kurt on Mom's lap, and I was fighting a losing battle against my eyelids. We slipped out the front door with several others.

Wig Taylor repeated his account of the final round and official results to congregated customers for months after. According to Wig this was what happened, and John Kinnan and Elmer Morris, the only customers left, verified his version.

At a little after midnight, Frank Tully ate his eighteenth hamburger to win the contest and then finished one more just because Becky had already prepared it, and he didn't want to seem impolite. Wimpy shook Frank's hand in sincere admiration and gave Wig four twenty-dollar bills for the whole works, including Turkey's share and a tip for Becky. He waddled out leaning on John and Elmer for support.

Wig also swears that right after Wimpy left the restaurant, Frank peered over the counter and, in an even higher-pitched voice, asked Becky, "You got any homemade apple pie back there? I've a taste for something sweet."

X

Swimming at DeGraff's Club Med

As a boy, I had several favorite places where I could disappear from one world and reappear in another. Loosely stretched down the hill behind our house, like the massive awning above Kinnan's Hardware, was Ernie's pasture field. Accessorizing the field was the Bokenghelas Creek, a liquid blue-green bunting attached to the pasture and running along its edges. The field and creek were my refuge, and Lady and I spent countless hours of our childhoods wading through both. In my adult life, I have looked for similar places for occasional hiding. I'm still looking.

Many small towns have a secluded swimming hole, and DeGraff was no exception. We had The Stump, the Club Med of DeGraff. After the Bokenghelas crawled through Ernie's pasture field and under the Mill Street Bridge, it slithered for a couple of miles more before disappearing into thick brush and undergrowth. I'd lose track of it at that point and had no interest in following it farther, knowing my creek eventually lost its pulse to the Great Miami River.

Along the passable route and downstream from the bridge, well out of sight from the road, the Bokenghelas pooled suddenly and deeply into a perfect swimming hole below the stump of a long-past oak tree. Judging from the stump's massive girth, the oak tree must have been huge. The fat basin of cool water beneath it looked out of place in the slender creek, like a ballooned aneurysm inflated to the bursting point at mid-artery. Our swimming spot could have been called The Pool as easily as it was The Stump, but for some reason it was always The Stump, and we never knew who named it or when. We just knew it had been used by the generation of boys before us and would remain pure for the generation after. The Stump had no beach, just a bare dirt bank about twenty feet long and four to five feet wide. That was enough for us. No one wanted to sunbathe when there was swimming to be done.

The deep, fully rounded middle served as our area for swimming. Other than where the creek spread itself peanut butter thin on either side of the actual swimming hole, there were no shallow parts. We had to be careful when wading into the ankle-high water because the deep part was quietly waiting to surprise us. No one knew how deep The Stump actually was, and I never touched bottom and didn't know any-one else who did.

Bellefontaine had a wonderful blue-colored, chlorinated pool at their City Park, a pool equipped with two diving boards, a water slide, and an area for water basketball and volleyball. But the Bellefontaine pool also had lifeguards with shrill whistles and multiple rules printed in big red letters posted all around:

NO RUNNING NEAR THE POOL
NO PUSHING OTHERS INTO THE POOL
NO BOTTLES AROUND THE POOL
NO UNSUPERVISED CHILDREN IN THE POOL
NO HORSEPLAY AROUND THE POOL
NO DUNKING OTHERS IN THE POOL

Cripes, they might as well have had a sign that read, NO FUN IN OR AROUND THE POOL DURING HOURS POSTED FOR SWIMMING!

At The Stump we had one unwritten rule, parent enforced and kid honored: "No swimming alone." That was it, and since the rule seemed like a good one, we obeyed it. I'm certain parents were a little concerned when their children said they were going swimming at The Stump and were equally relieved when their children came home safely, but over-protection never seemed to be an issue. My parents simply told me to be careful, and I always was.

The Stump was about as egalitarian as any place could be. In school we had our special cliques within the scholars, athletes, cheerleaders, band, chorus, FFA, 4-H, and gang of at-risk-to-dropout delinquents. My friends and I easily drifted in and out of each group except the last. Although those characters seemed okay, we usually avoided one another in school. But at The Stump, we were all unconditionally accepted. We were just a group of boys enjoying a swim.

The only time I actually got to know guys like Doc Manahan, Bill Greg, Chad and Brian Natham, and Ronnie Walker was at The Stump. Except for Doc, they weren't stellar students and usually seemed to be on or over the edge of trouble, spending as much time in the superintendent's office as in the classroom. According to Bill Greg during one of our man-to-boy Stump discussions, he was the smart one and not I.

"Why you want to be sittin' in class, twerp," he chided me, "when you can be sent to the superintendent's office and get a whiff of that hot Angle babe? Hell, I know she wants me."

And, hell, maybe Bill Greg was smarter than I gave him credit for. Marilyn Angle, the superintendent's secretary, was a definite babe. I was spending my school days with teachers like Mrs. Wammes, an excellent teacher but no Marilyn Angle. He had the Angle, and I had the Wambat.

At The Stump we talked a lot about girls, a whole lot about girls. The funny thing is I never saw a girl at The Stump, and none materialized no matter how much we fantasized. Maybe the tradition started out like a pirate ship rule where women were considered to be a curse and prohibited to go onboard. If they sneaked aboard, all kinds of disasters befell the ship and crew. Maybe we were simply avoiding Stump disasters. Other than that, I don't know why we were womenless. Because The Stump was a secluded area, I suppose some guys took their girlfriends there after dark, but except for skinny-dipping, I doubt much swimming occurred.

I learned about sex at The Stump. Dad had given me a junior birds and bees lecture early in my young life, but his nervous descriptions were pretty much textbook and biologically oriented. The big guys' pantomimes and monologues were more graphic than Dad's examples.

Later in life I discovered that Dad's accounts were more accurate but just not as interesting, while the big guys' purported deeds were fun to imagine but impossible to maneuver.

Harry Raymond "Doc" Manahan Jr. was the wild man of The Stump Club Med. Doc was a smoker, and "Doc the Camel Man" was our full nickname for him in honor of his favorite brand of cigarettes. He was labeled Doc because among his crowd he was the studious one, but Doc the Camel Man also fit him well.

Doc was the only one of us brave enough or indecent enough to swim completely naked. I can still picture Doc standing in native buff on top of The Stump, four lit cigarettes stuffed in his mouth, and clapping to get our attention before cannon-balling into the water's belly while flapping like a Dodo bird. He'd bob up quickly—the smoking gave him the worst breath-holding capacity among us—four soggy cigarettes dangling limply from his lips.

The rest of us laughed at Doc like it was the first time we'd seen his stunt, and Doc would splash around pretending to puff his Camels while lapping up our laughter. He spent a lot of money on cigarettes, feeding his habit and keeping us entertained, but I'm certain he thought the cost was worth it. I know we did.

As a kid, I never feared very much at The Stump, even though I suppose I should have. The only things that made me nervous were leeches and barbed channel catfish. But leeches were easily shriveled by sprinkles of salt, and I never suffered the sting of a catfish barb although Charles Tamplin did once. I'm certain the channel cats were more afraid of us than we were of them.

And none of us worried because The Stump didn't have lifeguards armed with whistles like they had at the artificial pool in Bellefontaine. We weren't concerned because we carefully guarded one another and saved our whistles for Doc.

THEY WERE RONG

They were rong
my teachers were.
Said If I quit sckool.
droped out.
Id never make it in the "real" world.
Im dum I no,
cant spell or read to good.
I tried but gess I was just cut out
to be a yellow bird fourever.
And I never could figger out
how it felt to be a dafadil in spring
or why they cared each fall
how I spent last summer.
And grammer, well my comas,
just never seemed to fit to good.
And run ons.
But I did good inmath
and I can count good.
At least Mr. Hinkle thinks so
thats why he hired me at the Sinclair station.
I make change ok
so I gess Im doin alright.
and I told Miss McGee my old English teacher
so when she stoped the other day for gas.
I just told her how this hear at the station
made more cents then all that other stuff.
and I think she believed me to
cause she didn't laff or nothing,
she just shook her head
and sorta cleared her throte.

XI

Ringers

His given name was Cleo, but in high school my Grandpa claimed a new name: Jack, after the boxer Jack Dempsey. When his parents asked why he changed his name, the budding pugilist answered, "Name one boxer named Cleo." Hearing no argument, he was Jack from that moment on.

Grandpa Jack loved boxing. Although I have never been an avid fan, I do remember watching Friday night fights on the *Gillette Cavalcade of Sports* with him. He could explain the specific strategies each boxer used better than the commentators and was able to predict, almost to the point, how the three judges were going to score the bout.

As a young man, Grandpa Jack boxed as a welterweight but never competed professionally or even semipro. A Golden Gloves program didn't exist in Lima during his prime, so he'd go to the downtown YMCA, work out with a local trainer, and box real rounds a couple of times a week against limited talent.

A tarnished silver trophy with a boxer in the classic stance crouched on the end table beside his easy chair. Grandpa Jack won the trophy by making it to the finals of a military tournament when he was in the Army, but he lost the championship match on a split decision and still complained, decades later, that he was robbed.

The trophy nameplate read:

RUNNER UP

WELTERWEIGHT CLASS

JACK "THE RINGER" GEYER

I once asked why he was called The Ringer, and he told me it was because when he wasn't on duty, he was usually in the camp's boxing ring working on his style. Then Grandpa Jack smiled, tapped me playfully on the chin with a soft right uppercut, and bragged, "Besides that, when The Ringer tagged his opponent, the guy heard ringing in his ears worse than Quasimodo."

I remember two distinct photographs of Grandpa Jack. In one he is posing as a boxer, the only time I ever saw him without a shirt. He had a wiry-lithe athletic build and swore his physique came naturally, because he never lifted weights or did serious workouts.

In the other photograph taken in November of 1917 at Camp Sherman in Montgomery, Alabama, he is in his Army uniform standing among the other infantrymen in the 37th Division. Grandpa Jack served in WWI with the 112th Supply Train. He'd never talk about the war, not even when I was doing a research paper in high school. The assignment was to interview a relative who had served in WWI or WWII, and I telephoned to ask about his experiences as a foot soldier. He said no, and at first I thought he was teasing me but quickly realized he was dead serious. He explained he had vowed never to relive the war and was not going to begin now, not even for me. I interviewed my father instead.

My brother Jeff has the picture of Grandpa Jack and his Army division hanging on a den wall. When I asked Jeff how he got it, he said he'd asked for it when he was helping my grandparents pack for their move back to Indiana. I'm glad he did. After Grandpa Jack's death and then my Grandma Ruth's a few years later, the relatives who lived close to them scavenged their possessions before the rest of us arrived. Not much was left to choose from, and I ended up with nothing, not even his tarnished trophy.

Grandpa Jack worked for a large oil refinery in Lima. When we'd drive for a visit and enter the city limits, I could see a towering smoke stack with a flame shooting out of it in the middle of the refinery. Grandpa Jack tested the oil's purity in an area beneath the flaming stack. I was proud to think he had such an important responsibility.

One evening during supper, my Uncle Richard called to tell us that Grandpa Jack had suffered a serious heart attack while splitting firewood. Mom and Dad drove to Lima and didn't return until late the next day. Grandpa survived, but the attack weakened his heart so much he couldn't do anything strenuous again and was forced to go on permanent disability, a major lifestyle change for him and my grandmother. He had, in the skip of a heartbeat, gone from an active vibrant man to an inactive sedate one.

The year after his heart attack, Grandma Ruth suggested they move back to Indiana to be closer to the children and grandchildren of her first marriage, and because of the move, our visits became less frequent. I missed them.

In Swayzee, Indiana, his life activities were reduced to simple routines. He'd arise early, eat a light breakfast, read the local and state newspapers front to back and again back to front, then take a nap until lunch. After lunch he'd drive to downtown Swayzee, flock with several newly found WWI buddies, and roost with them on a couple of large black wrought iron benches in front of a drugstore until returning home for supper. After supper, Grandma Ruth knitted while Grandpa Jack slept in his easy chair, the television on but entertaining neither. Bedtime, sunrise, and the cycle rewound itself again and again and again.

The downtown time with his friends was a daily highlight, and I think the conversations are what kept him going for so long after his first heart attack. The benches were known throughout Swayzee as the "Liars' Benches," and according to Grandpa Jack the veritable name was the only honest thing seated among him and his buddies. He claimed that no one should believe much of what was said by any of them. Truth was sprinkled sparingly throughout the endlessly respun yarns, and I gathered the point was never to let truth get in the way of a good story.

During our visits to Swayzee, Grandpa Jack sometimes let me tag along downtown with him. The first time I went I met Dusty Rhoades, the loudest of the liars flock. Grandpa Jack talked a lot about Dusty Rhoades and seemed to admire him. But to me old Dusty looked pretty much like the tail end of a misspent life.

Before we even shook hands Dusty asked me, in a menacingly raised voice, how it felt to be a grandson of the former welterweight champion of the Midwest. I didn't flinch at the size of the whopper Grandpa Jack had obviously spun to Dusty and his bench mates, suspecting Dusty was testing my loyalty as much as Grandpa Jack's veracity. Even at that young age, I knew family blood was thicker than the tedium of watered-down truth.

Their tall tale spinning was as contagious as chicken pox because I came down with a quick case of spinitis. With improvised, fast-action animation, I demonstrated to Dusty and the crew how Grandpa Jack taught me to set up a right-fisted uppercut knockout punch after a combination of sharp, piston-like left-hand jabs. I finished the story in a flurry of pugilistic prevarications and the boastful declaration that my sequence of moves was how Jack "The Ringer" Geyer knocked out Raymond "The Skipper" Ceylor for the welterweight title of the Midwest. Whew, what a whopper! Skip Ceylor was a classmate of mine whose name popped into my inventive little head.

After my performance, I reached out to Dusty Rhoades, shook his hand, and courageously declared, "Glad to meet you, Dusty. Want to go a few rounds?" A punching-bag pause filled silently with hot air before hard smacks of raucous laughter flattened it. Dusty slapped me enthusiastically on the back and announced, "Men, clear some room for this little guy. We got ourselves a liar in training." I squeezed in between Grandpa Jack and a hard-of-hearing cigar smoker named Fat Petey, satisfied that The Ringer's reputation was intact for at least one more card.

Bernie Jones was always thinking. I guess that happens when you sit in a wheelchair all day with nothing else to do. I could tell when Bernie had a brainstorm because as I sped down the hill toward his house with the daily *Examiner*, his shouts to me were an octave higher.

"Hurry up, Rickie, my boy, hurry up! Got an idea today!" I'd pedal faster so I could make a dramatic gravel-spraying stop a couple of feet in front of his chair. His ideas were usually impractical strokes of unimaginable invention, but I'd listen carefully before dashing his hopes. After all, he'd waited all day to tell me. In most cases my ears were opened, but my mind was mostly closed.

"What's the new idea this time, Bernie? What's going on in that head of yours?" Then, while lightly tapping on his head, I asked, "What's the abbreviation for mountain, Bernie?"

"Yeah, Rickie, it's M-T—empty—and you pulled that one on me a hundred times already. I'm serious now."

I could tease Bernie only so much. He needed someone to take him seriously, and most days I was his single willing candidate.

"You and your family play horseshoes, right?"

Where was this going? "Yeah, Bernie, we have a set, so what?"

"This Saturday after you deliver the papers, come back with the horseshoes and teach me to play."

Wait, whoa! The visual image of Bernie pitching a horseshoe was way beyond even my wild imagination. I mentally pictured a galloping horse throwing a shoe with more accuracy than Bernie pitching one, but I kept the spectacle to myself.

"Geez, Bernie, I don't know. I'd have to carry the horseshoes and the steel stakes over here on my bike, and I'd need a sledgehammer to whack the stakes into the ground. I don't think it'll work."

Sometimes you could successfully discourage Bernie, and other times you couldn't budge him with a forklift. This was a no budger.

"Come on, Rickie, please! My dad has a sledgehammer. Teach me horseshoes. Come on, Rickie, please!"

How do you say no to a guy with cerebral palsy and confined to a wheelchair? The idea was flimsier than a Three Stooges two-reel plot, but who was I to tell him it was goofy.

"Sure, Bernie, sounds like fun. We've got ourselves a date for horseshoes this Saturday."

That was on a Monday, and each day I delivered the paper during the rest of the week, I had an excuse made up for canceling our Saturday plans. And each day Bernie greeted me with something like, "Three more days, Rickie, my boy, three more days to horseshoes."

The clincher was Saturday afternoon when I delivered the paper, and he was wearing a brown cotton glove on his right hand. One gloved hand was not his style and way before Michael Jackson's fashion statement.

"Okay, Bernie, I'll bite. Why the glove?"

Bernie's teeth flashed yellow. "Rickie, my boy, I decided this will be my throwing hand. Mom says you got to be careful handling horseshoes. I'm protecting myself."

I had never considered if Bernie was right- or left-handed, and I doubt he knew for certain himself, but the gloved hand made him an official right-hander. As I prepared to open the paper and give Bernie his daily *Dick Tracy*, the gloved hand shooed me away.

"Just keep pedaling, Rickie, my boy. No time to waste. Big horseshoe match at the Jones house tonight!"

I finished the route and had a quick supper with my family. Dad helped me pack the four horseshoes and two metal stakes into his old Navy garment sack, making the load no more difficult than my regular newspaper bag. But I clanked more over the railroad tracks.

Bernie was waiting for me, a sledgehammer by his chair.

"I figure we have a couple of hours before dark, Bernie. I'll explain the rules while I set the stuff up."

I didn't know all of the official rules for horseshoe pitching, but rules weren't too important for this match. Bernie only had to know the basics. I explained that a ringer is worth three points, and if no one throws a ringer, the shoe closest to the post counts for one point. That was about all I knew. As I was hammering the stakes and yammering about the scoring, Bernie interrupted me.

"You're wasting time. Three points for a ringer, and one point for getting close. What are we waiting for?"

I pulled his chair beside the near post, and as we looked at the second post about ten yards away, I knew the moment of truth had arrived. How was Bernie going to hold a horseshoe, let alone pitch it? Bernie looked at me, and I looked at Bernie, and we spent several seconds looking at one another. I gave in first.

"Okay, Bernie, tell you what. For the first game I'll help you hold the horseshoe, and you and I will swing your arm together until you master the technique."

He accepted the concept, and that's what we did. For his first game of horseshoes, I did most of the holding and throwing for him. Gradually, he was able to gain a grip around the horseshoe, but he/we never came close to a post. After our shared throws, I'd pitch my own then wheel him to the opposite post. Back and forth we played, wheeling and walking, talking and laughing.

Twenty-one points wins the match, and I skunked Bernie twenty-one to nothing the first game. I tried everything to keep the score down and to get him some points. I threw left-handed. I closed my eyes. I even pitched behind my back show-off style, but I wasn't showing off. I just didn't want Bernie to feel humiliated. But fat chance of that happening because he was having the time of his life. Just before the second game, Bernie declared his independence.

"This game I throw the shoe myself. You help get it in my hand, but I do the rest."

"Oh, brother," I mumbled, half to myself and half hoping Bernie would hear my doubts.

I helped Bernie with his grip and moved behind him and to the left, satisfied I'd found a horseshoe safety zone. Silly me. Bernie wound up in his herky-jerky motion and the horseshoe released. I still have a crescent-shaped scar and slight bump on my shin, just above the right ankle, where the horseshoe thudded then ringed my foot.

"Dammit, Bernie!" I blurted without thinking. I had never sworn at him before, and the second the word slipped out of my mouth, I was sorry. But doggone it, that hurt!

Bernie cranked his head back and looked at the horseshoe ringing my foot.

"I don't suppose your leg counts as a ringer, does it, Rickie, my boy?" Through the pain of a throbbing shin, I managed to smile.

"No, Bernie, I can't give you any points for that one. Nice try."

Our second and third games also ended in skunks, and sunset was upon us. "Bernie, I need to get home before it's completely dark."

Bernie would hear none of it. "Rickie, my boy, you have a light on your bike. We still have time."

He was right. It wasn't as if DeGraff was a dangerous traffic town, even at night. The last bike versus car accident occurred in broad daylight a few years before when Lou Wigman, who rode his bike around town daily, ran into the back of Lafe Funk's pickup truck double-parked illegally in front of the post office. Crazy Lou limped into the post office and demanded that Auggie Leagre, the postmaster, drive him to Dr. Blank's office in the mail truck with yellow lights flashing. Auggie claimed he was too busy and told Lafe, who was waiting in line to buy stamps, to take care of Lou himself. Humiliated, Lou ended up being transported to the doctor in the back of the pickup truck that caused the assault in the first place, his banged up bicycle bouncing beside him. Both survived.

"Okay, Bernie, just one more game, then I need to go."

Halfway into the match we were both having trouble seeing either post through the vanishing light and quickly falling darkness. Finally, it was impossible to see a post directly in front of us, and the time to end our evening had come.

"One last throw, Bernie, and that's it." I gripped the shoe in his hand, and after feeling him tighten around it, I moved far to the right.

He twice swung his arm backward and forward in a labored, contorted 180 degree arch before the horseshoe let go. Neither of us saw the flight. And then came the most magical of sounds—metal hitting metal. Bernie gasped. I gasped.

I ran to the post and leaned down, looking and feeling at the same time. It wasn't a ringer. I could feel the rounded part of the horseshoe several inches from the post where it had struck and bounced back. I flipped the horseshoe quickly to collar it around the post.

"Rickie, is it a ringer? Is it a ringer?"

I hurried back and wheeled Bernie to the post. "Bernie, it's a ringer! You got a ringer! Your pitch was perfect, buddy, the best of the evening."

He was squinting his eyes and trying to see the horseshoed post. I grabbed his hand, and reaching down with his gloved hand in mine, we touched the ringed horseshoe together and captured his moment. Since high fives were not yet invented, our low five was enough.

After packing the shoes and posts back into the Navy sack, I wheeled Bernie to his front door.

"See you Monday, Bernie."

"See you Monday, Rickie, my boy." He paused a Bernie pause. "You know what? We don't have to play horseshoes anymore. I'm too good for you now."

I smiled at him. "Yeah, Bernie, you're too good for me now. See you Monday."

I whistled all the way home, but kept an eye out for Lafe Funk's truck.

XII

An Act of Comfort

My newspaper customers were an odd assortment who ranged from delightful to interesting to unique. I was genuinely awed by their eccentric diversity and grew to cherish them all, while trying not to show favoritism. But with Bernie, Fern, and Miss Lizzie, I did have favorites, and close to the top of that list was Mrs. Mary Waite.

Bryan and Mary Waite lived in a modest one-story house seated in the middle of a meticulously manicured, single acre of perfectly thatched Kentucky bluegrass and surrounded by well-populated rosebushes and intricately labyrinthed hedges. In his day Bryan Waite was famous around DeGraff for being a precisionist about his lawn and landscaping. My guess is he'd be diagnosed today as acutely compulsive.

Bryan Waite was also DeGraff's best furniture refurbisher, and no chair or couch was yard sale bound or beyond repair if it found its way into his expert hands. In all the years I delivered the paper, I never actually saw him in their house. He was either coiffing the greenery or busy in his neatly painted workshop connected to their house like a kite by a narrow pea gravel string of pathway. My mother's favorite chair once found its way down that path and into Bryan's workshop.

During a summer Sunday visit to my Uncle Ude's farmhouse when I was five or six, my mother rediscovered an antique Queen Anne chair. She remembered the chair, now languishing in Uncle Ude's attic-like storage space of a living room, from her childhood and expressed an interest in having it. Uncle Ude was a generous man and gave her the chair without hesitation.

I loved afternoons at my Uncle's homestead because he and his house were wonderfully unkempt and scattered: a roof-covered animation-like pigsty with occasional running water and almost bearable smells. I remember my mother once looking at the pile of dirty plates on the kitchen table and mockingly asking, "Ulys, do you ever put a dish away?"

He smiled his single-tooth smile while answering, "Sure I do, Dortha Jean, every time one of the cats licks a plate clean, I know it's ready for the cabinet."

The Queen Anne served as the resting place for a stack of well-worn *National Geographics*, at least two decades of post–World War I calendars, and a tattered Chinese checkers box filled with acorns. Uncle Ude scooped the chair dwellers into a large tin washtub, camping out by the chair and half-filled with corncobs and doorknobs, before hauling Queen Anne to our car. I swear I heard the squeal of a cat as the new occupants cascaded into the washtub, but I never actually saw it.

Mom delivered the chair, pretty much on its last Queen Anne leg, to Bryan Waite, and he worked his magic. He restored the chair to rose-petal newness, transforming her into the showcase of my parent's various living rooms for years to come. Bryan Waite was DeGraff's Rodin of wood and verdure.

His wife, Mary, was an invalid. The first couple of years I delivered papers to Mrs. Waite, I thought her invalidism was a treatable sickness, curable with proper medications and hearty helpings of homemade soup. I didn't understand why she never got better, so I asked Dr. Blank, DeGraff's only medical doctor and general practitioner, about her condition. He patiently explained that invalids like Mrs. Waite rarely improved, and the best medical prescription was to make them feel as comfortable as possible. I wanted to help however I could.

As it turned out, I was able to do something. Mrs. Waite made one simple, albeit unusual, request of me. She wanted me to read *The Bellefontaine Examiner* obituaries to her. Since Bernie Jones and *Dick Tracy* were the only other members on my oral interpretation list, I figured I could easily accommodate Mrs. Waite. She explained that her husband never read the obituary section, and she got depressed reading obituaries alone. I decided if my reading a few obituaries made her feel comfortable, that was the least I could do. Fortunately, she wasn't interested in the entire column, just the name, date and place of birth, and survivors.

I didn't read every day for Mrs. Waite as I did for Bernie. My cue was where she was located when I delivered the paper. If she was sitting outside and bonneted by the rose trellis her husband had built and nurtured daily for her, it was a reading. If she was waiting in a chair just inside the opened front door, it was a reading. When she was visible, I knew she was having a good day and up for the obituaries. On days I delivered the paper and she was nowhere in sight, she was having a bad day. Bryan Waite once explained to me, while meticulously styling the rose trellis, that on his wife's bad days, obituaries were too real for her.

Because Mrs. Waite took comfort in obituaries, I never felt morbid while reading them. Although she was an invalid—I never once saw her walk or even stand upright—she found something to be cheerful about with each obituary. If the person who died was older than she was, Mrs. Waite would smile and say, "I'm going to live to be older than that." If the deceased was younger than she, her response was, "I've already outlived that one!" Ironically, obituaries seemed to give her something to live for. The cycle of life continues even in death.

Children's obituaries were the exception to our reading rule, and the few I read made her sad. She'd whisper, "That is not right. That is just not right." I'd carefully refold the paper and place it gently on her lap before quietly leaving. When I finally came to realize that the obituaries of children were a discomfort to her, I stopped reading them. Although she never said anything to me, I suspect she was, after a time, on to my omissions. Children died, even in DeGraff.

Toward the end of my sophomore year in high school, Mrs. Waite's bad days began to outnumber her good ones. Our conversations were now brief, with me carrying the bulk of the talk. That spring and summer I saw her very few times. The last time I read to her, in early September, the trellised roses were surrounding her in full bloom.

Mrs. Waite died one balmy, spring-like late October afternoon, unusually nice weather for that time of year in Ohio. The next evening in the quiet of my bedroom, I slowly unfolded *The Bellefontaine Examiner* and read her obituary softly aloud.

Mary Ellen Sawyer Waite, born in 1902, is survived by husband Bryan. One daughter, Susan Elizabeth, died shortly after birth. Mrs. Waite was a lifelong resident of DeGraff and will be buried in Greenwood Cemetery.

I found comfort in the reading.

A COMPLEX CYCLE IN SIMPLE TERMS

Born
Weaned
Crawl, Walk, Talk
"Mommy," "Daddy"
Getting bigger
Growing up

Leave home
Off to school
New friends
Study
Graduation

"Hello, World"
Job; Success
Courtship
"I love you"
Marriage
Children
Raise them
Teach them
Watch them grow
Empty nest
Adjustments
"I love you"

Grandchildren
Hold them
Show them
Watch them grow
Retire
She dies.
Sadness
Alone
He dies.
Buried and gone

That quick
That complex
That simple
That's life

XIII

Watching Over from Above

Ohio thunderstorms blow up quickly. A day is hot and muggy, a few clouds congregate, caress, and then procreate by melting into one all-consuming, dark-roofed cloud. And, BOOM: a rainstorm and lightning show with surround sound.

One summer in the middle of August, several weeks before the start of a new school year, I had ridden my bike in sunshine to Hougen's garage to fold the newspapers, but rain began pouring before I could begin the route. The thunder kettledrummed while lightning stabbed downward in sharp parrying thrusts. John Slater, the Tamplin brothers, and I glanced at each other forebodingly as we watched the rain from inside the safety of the garage.

Each Christmas the fine folks at *The Bellefontaine Examiner* gave their underling carriers new waterproofed canvas bags as a gift for us to tote around their papers. The canvas bag had a flap to pull over the opening for the papers, and both sides of the bag had *BELLEFONTAINE EXAMINER* stenciled in capital bold blue letters. I figured all the free advertising I did for *The Examiner*, biking around DeGraff six days a week like a mobile billboard, should have been worth at least an extra buck or two, but what did I know? I was only a kid who annually wore out his canvas bag and was gifted a new one at Christmas. On this inclement August day, the waterproofed, flap-covered canvas bag was perfect for delivering papers, and I was grateful. I'd get soaked, but my freight would keep snug and bone-dry.

After we finished folding the papers, Charles and Herb decided to wait out the storm in the garage. Being the more adventuresome or foolhardy of the group, John and I decided we couldn't hold off any longer for the weather to break. Papers needed to be delivered, so we sloshed into the storm together, dragon tails of water sprouting behind our bike tires and tracking us. Lady loved the rain, although she wasn't too crazy about the thunder and lightning, and she ran beside me head up and tonguing the drops.

Delivering papers in the rain was one of my two least favorite activities. Delivering them on below-zero afternoons was the other. But being cold and wet was a natural way of life for paper carriers in Ohio.

Because of the driving rain, I couldn't just pitch the papers onto the porches as I usually did. Instead, I had to stop at each house and place the paper behind the screen door. Some customers even encouraged me to open their unlocked front doors and drop the paper inside. I saw some interesting sights during several of those unexpected door openings, but they will remain private.

The storm was torrential, and I was running way behind my regular schedule. Thoroughly soaked, I decided there was nothing I could do except keep pedaling and finish the route as quickly as possible. Luckily, I wasn't afraid of lightning, because hurled bolts were searing the sky from every direction.

As I skimmed toward the box factory, I thought I heard something through the thunder and pelting rain but wasn't certain. The sound was like the noise a large animal makes when it's been hurt. After I heard it again and then once more, I knew the source. Bernie!

"Help! Help!"

"My God," was all I could think, slicing through the rain, "what is Bernie doing out in this storm?"

As I passed the box factory and just before I cleared the railroad tracks, a flash of lightning lit the entire sky to the west, and I could see Bernie chaired in his side yard and framed against the white of his house like some gothic painting accessorizing an Alfred Hitchcock movie. I felt sick to my stomach. "What's going on here? What's going on?" I fumed aloud while racing faster. "This is crazy!" Bernie in his metal wheelchair, rain pouring down, lightning flashing all around—what was going on?

As I reached his house, I dumped my bike and papers in one motion and rushed up behind him. Bernie stared me a silent, "Where you been?" I pushed at his chair in a panic but my feet slipped, slamming my chin against one of the chair's metal handles. It didn't hurt, and I got better traction and began pushing Bernie to the front door as fast as I could manage. The door was closed, but the small overhang above it gave us protection. Lady shook herself, and the excess water created a pint-sized rainstorm before she flopped down.

"Bernie, what's going on? Where are your parents?" It was August, yet Bernie was snowy white, and his jaundiced teeth chattered a dead-of-winter chatter. He was too scared and saturated to speak.

I pushed the front door open and pulled Bernie inside. In all the time I'd known Bernie and delivered the paper, I had never been inside his house. I'd seen the kitchen from the doorway but hadn't been invited any closer. Although I still had not been invited, I was inside.

The kitchen was small with yellowed linoleum flooring and daisy-flowered wallpaper. Everything looked bright and surprisingly cheery except for the dark cabinets with even darker round knobs. The kitchen table had two chairs and an open space large enough for Bernie's chair. A dishtowel was folded neatly on the countertop, and everything was in its place with no dishes in the sink. Who knows why you notice what you notice, especially during dreadful times, but I remember every kitchen detail clearly.

I looked at Bernie to see if he was responding any better. He wasn't. Water dripped down his face from his soaked baseball cap, and I couldn't distinguish the rainwater from what I suspect were tears. He looked so helpless and humiliated, and I was angry.

"Where are your parents, Bernie?" I pried the cap from his head, pitched it into the sink, and grabbed the dishtowel to begin wiping his face and head. Still no answer.

"Bernie, I need a bigger towel, several towels. Where are they?" He jerked his head forward, and I saw a hallway and hurried over toward the first opened door. It was the bathroom, and I snatched three towels from a rack beside an old-fashioned freestanding bathtub. I massaged Bernie's head with one of the towels, determined to get at least part of him dry. After a minute or two, I changed towels and began again until his hair was only slightly damp.

"We've got to get you out of these clothes, Bernie," I said while pulling the white T-shirt pasted to his body up and over his head, then drying his back, arms, and chest. I was trying to figure out how to remove his lacquered pants when I noticed a line of plastic tubing stretched near his waist and disappearing down into the side of his pants above the belt.

I hadn't thought much about it before, but in those seconds I began to realize the daily struggles Bernie dealt with, struggles I could barely imagine. I didn't know how any of it worked for him, but I guessed functions routine for the rest of us were difficult for Bernie, and I didn't want to intrude upon his private life any further. He'd had enough humiliation for one day. I did my best to drape a dry towel over his shoulders, trying to cover his chest and give him warmth.

"I think we'd better keep your pants on, buddy, but let me take off your shoes and socks." I untied the laces, pulled off the shoes, and peeled away his white, wet, suctioned socks. I dried his feet as best I could, then pressed the towel against his legs and lap, trying to sponge away the remaining wetness.

"Bernie, I wish they made a giant squeegee for humans. Up your front, down your back, zip, zip, dry as a bone!" He still gave me no reaction.

I figured we needed some humor. "Come on, Bernie, you have to start responding." I then raised my voice, leaned into his face, and demanded, "Are you all right?" He nodded a slight yes. "No, Bernie," I corrected him. "You cannot be all right because half of you is left." I knew the joke was cornier than any of Flippo the Clown's lame lines, but I was getting desperate.

He managed a weak smile, and I finally felt some relief. Bernie was back. But just as suddenly, he looked panicked again.

"Rickie, you're bleeding! Your chin!"

I reached up, and sure enough I was bleeding and had bled quite a bit. The front of my shirt was sticky red and my chin felt syrupy. I looked like a messy little kid who'd chomped his way through a cinnamon red candy apple at the county fair. I went to the sink and dabbed myself with cold water. "Yeeow, that stings!" I didn't want to ruin a towel, so I packed a handful of napkins from the kitchen table against my throbbing chin.

I must have ripped the bottom of my chin when I slipped and hit Bernie's wheelchair, but in all the excitement nothing hurt until now. But now it really hurt. I felt dizzy and queasy from seeing my own blood, so I folded down to the floor by Bernie's bare feet. Had I been alone I would have cried, but not in front of Bernie. He'd been brave, and I wanted to be, too.

I clicked into slow motion as I cradled on the linoleum, chin throbbing and Bernie watching over from above. The throbs kept time with my heartbeat, and I closed my eyes to their rhythms.

Then, in one sudden and startling motion, the front door banged open, and Bernie's mom and dad rushed into the kitchen.

"Bernie!" his mother said, anguished. "Oh, Bernie, we are sorry. We are so sorry." She looked at me and saw the bloody napkins matted to my chin. "Rickie, you're hurt!"

"I'm okay, Mrs. Jones, really I am. Take care of Bernie."

Bernie's dad didn't say anything, but I could tell he was surveying the situation trying to figure out the chain of events. Finally, he spoke. "We had an emergency and had to leave in a hurry for Bellefontaine. No time to ask anyone to look after Bernie, but we thought he'd be okay. Damn rainstorm! The main road was flooded driving home, and we took a back road. Damn rainstorm!" Bernie's dad was a no-nonsense man, and this was difficult for him.

Glancing apologetically toward his wife and then to Bernie, he unflinchingly admitted, "She didn't want to leave Bernie by himself, but I insisted he'd be fine." He paused to breathe a slow breath. "I'm sorry this happened." His eyes shifted slowly to me. "Thanks, son."

I was no longer angry with either of them. Bernie's mom and dad looked ashamed, but I didn't know what to say to make them feel better. Nothing seemed right. I looked outside, and the rain had let up to a mist-like drizzle. "I'd better go. I still have the rest of my route to finish." I patted Bernie on the head and walked outside to my bike while they were both attending to him.

And there I saw the most horrible sight of an already horrid day. When I dropped my bike and newspaper bag in my haste to help Bernie, the newspapers had spilled out and scattered like pick-up sticks. They were waterlogged.

As I tried to stuff them back into the bag, I remembered I hadn't given a paper to Bernie or his parents. I grabbed one, ran back to the house, and handed Mr. Jones his dripping stick of ruined newspaper.

Then I started to cry, an uncontrollable sobbing cry. The pent up dam burst, and I flooded over. I was bawling.

"Come with me, son," Mr. Jones said, leading me out the front door. "I'm taking you home." I didn't protest.

Mr. Jones carefully laid my bike in the back of his pickup truck, gathered the soggy papers into the bag, and placed them on the floor in front of me. Lady jumped into the bed of the truck at his first command. I was gulping down little sobs, and we didn't speak during the drive.

The sun broke through the mist, and from my side of the windshield I caught sight of a rare double rainbow arched in the emerging blue sky beyond our house. I nudged Mr. Jones, and he looked before smiling down on me.

Mom and Dad came to the porch when they saw us pull into the driveway, but I stayed in the truck while Mr. Jones got out and spoke to them. I don't know why I stayed in his truck, but it felt safe. Finally, Dad opened the door and helped me out, rubbing my head like a puppy's. Mom looked at my chin and sucked breath through her teeth but stayed calm. They thanked Mr. Jones, and he left without saying anything else.

Mom drove me to Dr. Blank's office, and he cleaned the wound and sewed in eighteen stitches. I still have crisscross scars on my chin. Dad and Jeff finished my route, taking the papers to each customer and explaining what had happened. Dad later told me that most of my customers weren't too upset, and I remember hoping there wasn't much important news happening in the world or Logan County in that edition.

Mr. and Mrs. Jones never mentioned the incident to me, and Bernie and I didn't talk about it either. Some adventures aren't fun to relive.

But after that day, every time I collected for a week with a holiday in it, Mr. Jones gave me the extra nickel. I took it gratefully and stuffed it in my left front pocket with the others.

LONG AGO

I once, long ago, heard grass
sigh and sing
as it furled in the wind.
I saw it spring with rain
and wave to clouds.
And I would cry when green turned brown
and living turned withered
and ground turned barren.
But that was long ago.

I once, long ago, sat nose to nose with flowers
and smelled their glory
and stroked their plumage
and rubbed their pollen
and laughed aloud back to them.
And I would cry when, one by one,
they stripped bare and slouched,
nude heads downward.
But that was long ago.

I once, long ago, made friends with trees
and rode them piggyback
and borrowed their arms for slingshots and bows.
I sat by their feet and heard their stories,
and they listened to mine.
And I would cry when green turned brown
and arms turned bare
and trees turned silent.
But that was long ago.

Long, long ago
in a simple childhood world
of grass and flowers and trees.

Now,
I sometimes stand by my window
and watch the rain
and wish I could cry.

XIV

Men of Good Humor

During our early years in DeGraff, my father directed the choirs in several different Protestant churches. As a family, we were faithful church attendees, although the particular church we attended was seldom consistent from one year to the next. However, when I was in the sixth grade, the DeGraff Methodist Church became our permanent place of worship.

The basement of the Methodist Church was used to host a variety of functions, and among my favorites were the potluck dinners after church and the evening suppers before special programs. Each church woman had her specialty dish, and to this day I can still taste my buffet-line choices: my mother's baked beans; Goose Roby's shredded chicken sandwiches; Mag Comer's sugar-cured ham and candied yams; Suzie Heintz's German potato salad; Frances Tamplin's fudge-layered chocolate cake; Nannette Wren's graham cracker pudding; and Jinny Knief's double custard cream pie. Cruise ship cuisine is not their equal.

The Cub Scouts and Boy Scouts held their weekly meetings in the church basement. Jeff and I were scouts, and I'm certain Jeff still shares a record with Bob Smithers for the longest sustained laugh during a formal Cub Scout induction ceremony.

Bob Smithers, one of the high school science teachers, served as scout master for our Cub Scout and Boy Scout troops. He was a stickler for formality, especially during solemn ceremonies. The year Jeff was inducted, Bob decided that having each young scout recite a line of the official *Scout Pledge* would be more impressive than the scout master reading the whole thing himself. Each inductee was to memorize an individual line and then repeat that line as he lit a smaller candle from the larger "Source of Truth and Light" candle.

Jeff was assigned the last line, "…and Cub Scouts prepares us for adulthood." The line was simple, and Jeff had no problem memorizing it. For the entire week leading up to the ceremony, Jeff cleverly incorporated the line into his bedtime prayers, giving him extra practice and heavenly insurance. With one line and lots of practice, we figured there was no way for Jeff to mess up. As it turned out, we were all far too optimistic and should have given Jeff more credit.

Dad was seated in the front row poised with our box-shaped Brownie Hawkeye Camera to snap Jeff's big moment. As Jeff lit his candle, he smiled proudly at Dad and delivered his line, "…and Cub Scouts prepares us for adultery." Jeff and the other innocent cubbies had no idea why his words were met with gales of laughter, torrents of laughter. I couldn't believe my ears, Mom smothered her face, and shaking with a convulsive horselaugh I'd never heard erupt from him before, Dad flashed a perfect picture of his right foot.

After a couple of minutes, the laughter still had not subsided and tears cascaded down adult faces. Bob Smithers, seeing his well-planned candlelight ceremony going up in flames, stood and waved his arms as if to plead for some semblance of decorum.

After we quieted to a few restrained titters, Bob delivered the *coup de grace*. "Well, friends, if Cub Scouts prepares these lads for adultery, one can only imagine what's in store for our Boy Scouts."

Point, set, match, and the evening, for all intents and purposes, was over. More laughter exploded, and a new comedy team of Bob Abbott and Jeff Costello was the talk of the town throughout the following weeks. Jeff, God bless him, still got his Cub Scout pin and eventually became a Boy Scout troop leader. I cannot attest to his fidelity in later years.

My youngest brother, Kurt, also had his moment of glory during a program in the Methodist Church basement. One Wednesday evening the elementary Sunday school classes performed a dramatization of several biblical parables, and in one of the scenes Kurt was cast in the role of a sandal maker. After two king-sized sheets used for curtains were pulled apart along a clothesline extended wall to wall, Kurt and a couple of other sandal makers were visible, sitting on a long bench and cobbling with wooden mallets. Kurt didn't have any lines, so my family and I had no reason to be nervous.

At events like this, the majority of the audience members were parents and other family members. Giving up the prime part of a Wednesday evening was serious business in DeGraff. A few other church members usually attended as a courtesy, but most of us had a relative on the portable wooden stage. Jeff and I were in attendance out of enforced loyalty and not because we were overly excited about watching Kurt and the other amateur squirts perform.

Seated in the middle of the front row of folding metal chairs, elbows on his knees and hands cradling his chin, was Frank Tully. Frank seldom missed any type of social event in DeGraff, and he certainly never missed an event at the Methodist Church. A lifelong member of the church, he reportedly had not missed a service in decades. Frank Tully was the Lou Gehrig of the DeGraff Methodist Church, our homegrown model of loyal perseverance.

During the famous blizzard of 1950, a freak snowstorm blanketed and paralyzed most of Ohio, and no one ventured outside for days. Roads in and around DeGraff were impassible, and all of the town sidewalks were blocked with several feet of snow. Bob VanBuskirk missed his daily route delivering Hopewell Dairy milk around DeGraff, house to house, for four consecutive days. Kenny Fuson's IGA ran out of food because his suppliers from Columbus were unable to access their warehouses. Even the rural mail went undelivered despite the weathered creed of the post office and its noble carriers.

Frank Tully, DeGraff's hamburger-eating confirmed bachelor, lived on Cretcher Street several blocks from the Methodist Church, and each Sunday he'd briskly walk to church. But there would be no need for him to walk to church the Sunday of the great blizzard. In fact, there would be no church service at all because for the first time in church history, the service was cancelled. The minister at the time was Reverend Howard Householder, a man of good humor, who posted the words on the church marquee by the front entrance: CHURCH CANCELLED THIS SUNDAY. HELL FROZE OVER.

But no one thought to inform Frank Tully, and he didn't see the posting until he had waded through several sidewalks and plodded toward the church's front doors, fitted with a pair of snowshoes he hadn't worn since his winter walks to the DeGraff School almost five decades past. I cannot begin to imagine Frank's combined surprise and disappointment at having journeyed to church in such impossible conditions only to discover the service was cancelled. According to Reverend Householder's wife, Thelma, who was watching from a window in their home beside the church, mounds of snow scattered as Frank opened the church's massive oak doors and high stepped inside.

Mrs. Householder told the Reverend about Frank, and together they watched for him to leave the church. When he emerged, again opening the doors wide and scattering more snow, they called out to him from their front door and invited him to come inside for a cup of coffee. According to Reverend Householder during his sermon the following Sunday, of which Frank Tully was the topic, Frank smiled but turned down their invitation. "Sorry, Reverend and Mrs. Householder, but I've got a deep walk home. I enjoyed the sermon today, Reverend. Your best one in years!" Reverend Householder wasn't the only man of good humor in DeGraff.

During church services Frank Tully always sat in the first pew, directly in front of the pulpit and the minister. His distinctive high-pitched voice stood out from the collective voices of the rest of the congregation, but even more so because his responses were invariably a word behind everyone else's. He was a word behind during the Apostle's Creed, the Lord's Prayer, the Words of Response, and every verse of every hymn. It was maddeningly distracting, and oftentimes I'd find myself following Frank's vocal lags instead of being led by the minister.

But because Frank Tully was so blessed sincere, no one ever faulted him or requested him to join in unison with the rest of us. Like the day of his snowshoed, singular sojourn to church to worship alone, Frank was out of step with the rest of DeGraff. Or maybe it was just the other way around. Maybe Frank Tully was the only one in step and the only one with the proper cadence and rhythm. Maybe all the rest of us were out of step and too fast by one word. I don't know. I do know that every church needs a Frank Tully. Every church needs a person of conviction who sits down front and leads by following.

So, it was no surprise to see Frank Tully in attendance at the Sunday school's elementary student performance of biblical parables, sitting in the middle of the front row with his elbows on his knees and his hands cradling his chin.

But it was a surprise, a big surprise, when the head of Kurt's wooden mallet flew off in mid-swing, somersaulted through the air, and banged off Frank's bald head before landing at his feet. Frank was wounded and Kurt was pained, but Jeff and I were the ones in stitches.

After an awkward moment of suspended cobbling, Kurt stood, bounded off the platform, and hurried out to Frank. While rubbing the growing red welt atop his smooth head, Frank had already reached down for the mallet top and put it in the pocket of his favorite, and only, plaid cardigan sweater. Frank must have thought he'd won himself a door prize or something because when Kurt stretched out his hand to Frank, palm up in silent request for the top of his prop, Frank happily shook Kurt's hand and thanked him.

Kurt stood bewildered until Mrs. Shawan, the director for the evening's entertainment, called for him to return to the stage. He stepped back onto the platform and began to cobble once again, this time with a headless stick, but he was not a good enough actor to conceal his lost zest and thespian enthusiasm. The scene was tough to watch, but Kurt managed to fake his way through the crafting of a sandal. His bow at the parable's conclusion was half-hearted.

We were consoling Kurt while walking to our car when Wynn and John Kinnan, father and son partners in Kinnan's Hardware, approached us. John's daughter had been a stable maid in one of the scenes. John and Wynn Kinnan never missed an opportunity to needle my father, who was known throughout DeGraff for his legendary tool ineptitude. Anytime Dad entered their store to buy hardware or to ask for handyman advice, he'd end up being the punch line to a Kinnan joke or impromptu comedy routine. Always the good sport, Dad was an even better foil.

"Hey, Lewie," John chuckled, "looks like Kurt's a chip off the old block the way he handled his mallet tonight." John knew full well that Dad could barely handle a hammer himself. We all managed weak smiles, except for Kurt, who was trying to figure out if John was complimenting him or not.

Wynn never let his son have the last line. "No, John," Wynn cut in, "after seeing the knot on poor old Frank's shiny head, it looked more like a Kurt chip shot off the old block."

Even though Kurt didn't understand Wynn's golf analogy, he laughed along with the rest of us and seemed to feel better. Dad remained silent and in deep thought during our drive home.

The following weekend my father vowed to teach my little brother the art of carpentry. That was quite a concept: Dad the master builder with Kurt as his apprentice. They decided to build Lady a doghouse, and the entire weekend was spent measuring, sawing, and hammering. After they finished their work, Kurt nailed a neatly printed sign—LADY'S PALACE— just above the square-oval-triangled front opening. I never once saw Lady enter her palace, but I don't think that was my father's point. The contorted kennel stood crookedly proud as a monument to his sense of humor.

Toward the end of the week, after word about the project had passed throughout the town, John and Wynn Kinnan stopped by our house to view the construction. As he looked at Lady's doghouse, John Kinnan was, for once, speechless.

After a slow, chin-scratching walk around it and careful inspection, Wynn looked at John and then toward my father before breaking the silence. "Well, Lewie, I'll give you credit for one thing. That sign is spelled perfect!"

XV

Canvas-Caped Phosphorescent Man

Danny Coonzy lived catty-corner from us, and Steve Houchin's house was one block over from Mill Street. The three of us were friends even though Steve and Danny were exact opposites, and Steve didn't like Danny very much. Steve was athletic, assured, and smart, and after graduating from high school with a perfect 4.0 grade point average, he was awarded a scholarship to attend Ohio State University. Danny was chubby, vulnerable, and struggled in each grade to make it to the next. Life never offered him any scholarships. If it hadn't been for his grandparents, Danny would not have experienced a family at all. I liked Steve and Danny both, but being friends with Danny took extra effort.

Danny Coonzy had a difficult home life. His parents were either together and unhappy or separated and unhappy. Danny learned well from them, and as a consequence, he was an equal mixture of sullen and moody, making him a challenging guy to be around. When we were kids, his parents moved to Hoboken, New Jersey, and left Danny to be raised by his grandparents, Dolph and Mamie Coonzy. Then, when he was in the sixth grade, they came back in the middle of the night and pirated him off to Hoboken to share their misery.

In the hemisphered world of Danny Coonzy, people were divided into two groups: those who were pot-lickers and those who were not.

If Danny was mad at you, you were a pot-licker. If Danny was in a bad mood, you were a pot-licker. His parents were always pot-lickers. Steve Houchin and I were usually pot-lickers. Dolph was sometimes a pot-licker, and Mamie was never a pot-licker. Danny's world was pretty pot-licking defined.

Danny Coonzy had an interesting phobia. While some people are abnormally afraid of snakes, spiders, crowded elevators, heights, leaving the house, germs, the number thirteen, black cats, and broken mirrors, Danny was afraid of fireflies, the lightning bug insects that glow in the dark. Every time my brother Jeff and I excitedly captured fireflies at dusk by hand-cupping them into grass-layered mayonnaise jars with punctured tin lids, Danny would stand protected inside the safety of his front porch screen door and yell at the top of his lungs that we were pot-lickers. Jeff and the lightning bugs didn't seem to mind, but it kind of hurt my feelings. Danny needed a friend, and not many other kids in DeGraff applied for the job, so I was pretty much it for him, pot-licker or not.

One summer day, Danny and I planned a campout for that evening within the dangers of the vast wilderness—my backyard. We pitched a tent by throwing one of Dad's large paint tarps over Mom's back-yard clothesline, then weighed down the imperfectly formed triangle with bricks along each side. If Daniel Boone had known about Mom's clothesline, Dad's canvas tarp, and Danny's and my comforts, his trek to founding Boonesborough wouldn't have been as challenging. With thick blankets, soft pillows, and plenty of RC Cola and potato chips, Danny and I were hunkered down for our night in nature.

We tucked ourselves in with some help from my mom and his Granny Mamie, then sloshed down potato chips with gulps of RC while reading *Superman* and *Batman* comic books by flashlight. After the batteries and we began to fade, we drifted off to peaceful sleep, the tarp's scent of turpentine and oil-based paint hardly bothering us.

In the middle of Danny's mini-snores and well into the deep of night, about 9:30 p.m., a scoundrelly little brother sneaked into the tent and strategically filled our triangle bedroom with fireflies he'd captured earlier in the evening. He knew Danny's phobia, and he knew he was being a bratty brother. Yes, he knew all of that, and that is why Jeff delighted in the treachery.

Poor Danny! As he thwacked his manifest phobia, the fireflies burst and gilded his exposed body parts. Where Danny had skin, he had firefly squish. The more he swatted, the more the innocent fireflies smeared and glossed him head to foot. He finally cracked and crazily scrambled out of our makeshift tent, the tangled tarp entwined around him.

And there went Danny, tent in tow and trailing him like a Transylvanian wedding train, a giant lightning bug himself glowing in the night and flitting across the street to the safety of his house while arousing the neighborhood with his serial screams of "pot-lickers." He'd been transformed into the newest supernumerary comic book action figure: Canvas-Caped Phosphorescent Man! Pot-licker Jeff, finishing Danny's bag of potato chips, enjoyed the moment.

One early spring, Steve, Danny, and I decided to build a raft. We each had a seaworthy title and specific duties as assigned by Steve, who designated himself the captain. I was first mate and navigator, while Danny was relegated to crew and head deck swabber. Danny was just happy to be welcomed aboard and, for once, didn't complain.

Down the hill from our house was the Bokenghelas, an almost creek named after the last of Ohio's Shawnee Indian Chiefs. The Bokenghelas was truly mild, but that didn't matter to me. I loved the creek and spent many hours wading in it, skipping flat stones on it, and fishing futilely in youthful bliss. But floating a raft on the Bokenghelas was my ultimate dream.

The box factory manufactured cardboard boxes of all shapes and sizes and shipped their products nationwide on wooden skids. We salvaged and dismantled several skids from the factory and banged out a splinter-infested, almost-flat raft and then strapped two inner tubes to the bottom. After nailing on an in-name-only rudder, we carried her proudly down to the Bokenghelas.

In honor of Danny's Granny Mamie, who frequently treated us to homemade brownies and ice cube tray Kool-Aid popsicles stabbed with toothpicks, we named our raft *The Mame*. Granny Mamie was proud of her namesake, and she whacked a bottle of RC Cola on her as a christening before our official launch. The bottle wouldn't break against the raft's soft wood, no matter how hard she whacked, but none of us knew better anyway. We thought the ritual was a fitting tribute to our many anticipated journeys.

Granny Mamie packed peanut butter and jam sandwiches for us to enjoy on our maiden voyage. Because Tupperware was either not yet invented or hadn't made its way to DeGraff, the sandwiches were wrapped in waxed paper and transported in a Fuson's IGA grocery bag. We soon discovered that creek-soggy peanut butter and jam sandwiches are barely edible.

We were all a bit too euphoric about our maiden voyage. The creek was too shallow, the inner tubes too few, and three of us too heavy. We launched, hit bottom, and sat wet and motionless while the water curled around us in giggling ripples. We ended where we started.

We shouldered the raft back to our storage shed for future adjustments never made, and she was soon forgotten among the many other dreams of young boys during a short spring and long Ohio summer. I suspect my creek still awaits the conquerors.

Danny's parents hauled him off to Hoboken the following year, and I didn't see him again until a couple of decades later when he attended a regional Kiwanis meeting in Kent, Ohio, and found my name in the local telephone book. He was a tool salesman for an outfit selling merchandise town to town out of paneled trucks.

At dinner that evening I heard Danny's post-DeGraff history. He'd been married and divorced three times and had children he'd lost contact with, although he did have a billfold full of baby pictures. During dinner he referred to each ex-wife and a couple of Coonzy progeny as pot-lickers, and I noticed his pot-licker adjectives had become more profane since childhood. Even though he bragged he'd finally met the perfect woman at an Atlantic City casino and was thinking of marrying again, he still seemed to be an equal mixture of sullen and moody. I forgot to ask if Hoboken had fireflies.

Thinking back on it, I'm glad Steve Houchin and I were friends with Danny. A guy needs at least two friends at some point during his pot-licking life.

A FIGMENT OF MY YOUTH

Below the hill
on which our house was throned,
in my hometown,
trickles a creek.
In my youth I fancied
the creek to be most remarkable
and filled with enchantment, excitement,
history, mystery, and life.
I often visualized bloody pirate ships
besieged in battle upon those waters,
or sneaking German submarines slithering below them.
I often imagined many famous explorers
using my creek for passage to their quests
and carrying back tantalizing tales
describing the great white waterway.
And I was certain that my creek,
on a permanent peregrination,
had gone far, seen much,
delighted many, and disappointed none.
It even housed crayfish,
gigantic creatures with gigantic claws,
for me to wade after
even though I privately
hoped never to catch one.
Yes, I fancied my creek
to be most remarkable
in my youth.

I returned to my creek
after years and miles had removed me.
So different now
though actually unchanged:
shallow—no more than two feet deep;
steady—coming from nowhere and returning soon;
silent—currents hardly even murmuring.

I caught a crayfish
in an old coffee can
and watched it
scamper frantically
round and round and round
until I let it go
unharmed.

XVI

Carnival Coming to Town!

CARNIVAL COMING TO TOWN!

CARNIVAL COMING TO TOWN!

CARNIVAL COMING TO TOWN!

My brother Jeff and his best friend, Mike Bodenmiller, were always in the middle of something, and this time they landed themselves something productive. A man named Big Red, the manager and advance man for a traveling carnival headquartered in Sarasota, Florida, had arrived in DeGraff a couple of days before his troupe to check out our downtown for the carnival setup.

While Big Red was walking up and down Main Street with a clipboard and sketching out locations for the various rides, booths, and tents, Jeff and Mike, always the curious pair, stopped him to ask what he was doing. After a quick explanation, Big Red hired them both on the spot to nail "Carnival Coming to Town" posters on every telephone pole in DeGraff. He gave each of them a dollar bill, and they strutted around like they had suddenly become Rockefellers.

Big Red furnished a box of two-penny nails, a claw hammer, and an armload of posters, and he designated Jeff to be the hammerer and Mike to be the supplier. He said Jeff looked like he could handle a hammer, quite an honor for one of Lewie Niece's boys. Since Jeff eventually went into construction for his livelihood, Big Red turned out to be almost as prophetic as the Gypsy fortuneteller who traveled with the carnival and peered into my mother's future.

During the middle of the carnival's week-long run, my mother decided to have her fortune told. Mom was pretty excited when, inside a colorful tent propped up in front of the DeGraff Public Library, the Gypsy looked into her crystal ball (Mom later said it looked more like a big glass ornament from one of the posts on an old four-poster bed), fluttered her eyes rapidly for several seconds, and dramatically announced that Mom would soon be coming into a large inheritance. Her philanthropic prophecy cost only fifty cents.

Two weeks later in an act of coincidence or predestined fate—who really knows about these things—my mother's Uncle Ed died in Lima. A couple of days later she received word he'd left her two hundred and fifty dollars. It didn't matter how anyone else quantified what the Gypsy meant when she predicted a large inheritance, two hundred and fifty dollars was a tidy sum for my mother, and she considered it to be huge. After her evening of good fortune, Mom became a "you *can* see into the future" convert, and now trusts fortune cookies for their prophetic messages.

The carnival caravan arrived in DeGraff early on a Saturday morning, packed into several large semi-truck trailers and pickup trucks. An Airstream mobile home linked within the procession served as Big Red's home and the carnival's headquarters. He parked his rig near the alley running beside Andy Stayrook's Auto Sales, and Andy was one of the first customers on my paper route. Big Red's path was about to cross with another one of Lewie Niece's boys.

When I delivered my papers on Saturday afternoon, Big Red was standing beside his Airstream barking orders at two little guys who didn't look much older than I was. They were trying to carry a large rope but making a mess of it. The long length of rope—the fat, thick kind used on boats and docks—was tangled and twisted into several oval loops, and the two of them were tripping while groping the rope, thoroughly entwining themselves into the jumble more than they were capturing it. I'd never seen a boa constrictor engulf its helpless victim, but this was pretty close to how I imagined the scene would look. Big Red wasn't happy.

"What the hell is wrong with you two? Are you complete idiots? I don't know why I let your uncle talk me into hiring on either one of you in the first place. You both register record high on the worthless meter!" Big Red stopped to take a breath, causing his face to inflate even bigger and redder. He was a quick breather and began again immediately.

"If we don't get this rig up and ready in time for opening tonight, I'm holding you two numbnuts responsible. And when we pull out, I swear to God I'll leave you both behind to rot in this hick burg. That'd teach you a lesson. How'd you like to be left behind here?"

The boys shook their heads side to side in nervous, rapid motions. Then, moving their feet faster than the tap dancers on Ted Mack's *The Original Amateur Hour*, they hoofed their way down the street toward the center of town, skipping rope in tandem every couple of steps. Big Red mumbled something unintelligible and walked back toward his trailer.

"Hey," I yelled before he opened the door, "this isn't a hick burg, this is DeGraff. And if you left them here, they wouldn't rot. People take care of one another here."

Big Red's thick, red neck swiveled his red-haired head and even redder face back in my direction. The glare he shot made me stumble back a step, but I courageously regained my ground and even moved a couple of more feet in his direction. Who was this guy to bully little kids and insult DeGraff?

"And who might you be?" he asked. As he looked me up and down, I felt like I was being measured the way Matt Dillon measures the doomed gunslinger at the beginning of each *Gunsmoke* episode, but I wasn't afraid. Hometown loyalties run deeper than fear.

"My name is Rickie, and I live here. You hired my brother, Jeff, and his friend a couple of days ago to nail your posters around town."

Now those were words of pure desperation. I could have said a dozen different things to answer who I was, but I chose to mention Jeff's name to validate me. It seemed to work, and Big Red lightened. Everyone liked Jeff, and by association most people liked me.

"Sorry, fella, I didn't mean to disrespect your town. Me and the carnival are glad to be here. It's just that those two little runts mess up whatever assignment I give them. Carrying rope is the easiest thing to do around here, and they even screw that up. But what the hell, I suppose they'll learn soon enough."

As Big Red talked, I carefully measured him as he had measured me. The source of his name was obvious. His hair, face, neck, ears, hands, and arms were all bright red. Eric the Red would have been reduced to Eric the Pink beside this guy. He also looked weathered and aged beyond his years. Carnival life probably does that to you, and I figured he started traveling when he was about the same age as the two young rope wranglers.

He noticed *The Bellefontaine Examiner* canvas bag stuffed with papers hanging over my shoulder.

"You deliver the local paper?" he asked, motioning his red chin toward the bag.

"Yes, I do. This is *The Bellefontaine Examiner,* and the newspaper covers all of Logan County plus state, national, and international news." Cripes, I sounded like a promotional banner printed above the daily headlines.

"Got an extra copy?" he cut in, obviously not interested in *The Examiner*'s range of coverage.

"Sure, it costs a nickel," I answered while reaching into my bag for the extra copy I carried for opportunities like this. I handed the paper to him like a kind of peace offering. I didn't know why I cared for his approval, but I did. I guess I felt like I was representing the whole town at that moment and wanted Big Red to know DeGraff was a good place to live. We weren't just any burg.

"Tell you what, fella, give me the paper each day, and I'll pay you in full before we pull out. I like doing business with you. Deal?" He stuck out his beefy red hand and engulfed mine with the shake. "My name's Big Red," he said proudly during the mid-shake of a hard squeeze. "Glad to meet you, fella."

"Yeah, I know your name. My brother told me about you, and like I said before, my name's Rickie."

As I was getting back on my bike, Big Red reaffirmed our deal. "Just leave the paper on the steps of this trailer. I live here. We got a deal, fella?"

"Sure, we've got a deal," I called back while pitching Andy Stayrook's paper perfectly on his small front porch.

Big Red made our deal sound official, kind of like he and fella were now business partners.

As I delivered the rest of my papers, I kept thinking about how lucky I was. I liked having a hometown and a family. I liked the notion of living in one place, eating Mom's cooking, sleeping in my bed, and having a fully stocked drawer of clean underwear and socks for daily changes. The image of the two boys struggling with the rope stuck with me, and I wondered if they were brothers, what happened to their parents, and how an uncle had the authority to give them to Big Red and the carnival?

Some of my friends, especially Paul Whitehead, often pined on about running away and joining a circus. Paul's dream was to be like the character Corky on *Circus Boy*, a Saturday morning TV show. Corky was a kid about our age played by Mickey Braddock, who in real life grew up to be Mickey Dolenz of the group The Monkeys. Paul tried his best to talk Ned Heintz and me into jumping on a train by the box factory with him and finding a circus to join, but the idea never appealed to us. When we were in the sixth grade, Paul missed school for a week, and Ned and I figured he had run off to seek his circus fame. We later found out he'd had his tonsils removed.

After my encounter with Big Red and delivering the rest of my route, I rode my bike back through the center of downtown to check out the various booths and rides. Everything was scheduled to open at 7:00 p.m. that evening. Main Street was blocked off from North Main at the Methodist Church all the way to the railroad tracks on South Main, just past the Sinclair Gas Station. This was the first real carnival to hit DeGraff in years, and it was definitely the first one in my lifetime.

I was excited and had been saving extra money throughout the summer. I stuffed over twenty dollars away and planned to blow it all on rides, games, and junk food.

My girlfriend at the time was Joyce Hengsteler, a ninth grader, and I was justifiably proud to be dating an older woman. I was an eighth-grade junior high student, and with Joyce being in high school, I was the envy of my friends, at least as far as the guys were concerned. The girls in my class didn't seem too impressed.

Joyce was out of town with her parents during the first part of the carnival's run, so I planned on going stag. We agreed to go together later in the week, and she made me promise not to take any of the really fun rides without her, especially the Ferris wheel.

Everything looked almost in place as I pedaled up and down the sidewalks of Main Street and watched the roustabouts finishing their particular jobs. I carefully eyed the food concessions and planned my supper before biking back home. My meal was going to be an Italian sausage sandwich with plenty of hot peppers and no onion, boardwalk French fries with vinegar, funnel cake sprinkled generously with powdered sugar, and a giant cup of fresh lemonade to wash everything down. Looking at the prices posted on the front of each food stand while doing the mathematical additions in my head, I knew I could buy all the nourishment I craved for about $2.00. Like my dad, I was a bargain hunter.

I hurried home and counted the minutes until 7:00 p.m. Mom and Dad decided it'd be nice for all of us to go to the carnival as a family, and I was okay with the plan. As long as my parents tagged along, Jeff and Kurt wouldn't be too much of a nuisance. Mom approved of my carnival junk food choices, and Dad paid for it. I hadn't brought much money with me, saving the real spending for my time with Joyce, so Dad's offer to treat was a nice surprise.

I'm a sucker for games of chance, and I think the fascination started with that first carnival in DeGraff. Carnival hucksters are smooth talkers who know how to egg you into spending hard-earned cash at their booths. Promises of "you can't lose" and "this is so easy your kid sister can do it" are not easy to resist, especially if you're a guy who wants to look heroic in front of his girlfriend. No carny pitch was good enough to entice my dad, however, and he wouldn't let me spend a quarter on any of the temptations. Since I'd have time on my own to win my share of Kewpie dolls, stuffed animals, and big straw hats, I agreed.

The evening with my family was a good one, and because we enjoyed watching Kurt have fun, even Jeff and I got along without any shenanigans between us. We rode the safe rides, and I kept my promise to Joyce by saving a couple of the more daring rides and the Ferris wheel for her.

Mom liked the merry-go-round, and we all went around with her and Dad three times. Dad even nabbed a brass ring allowing Mom and him to ride a fourth time for free. I stood between Jeff and Kurt, holding their hands, and the three of us watched the two of them climb onto the same large horse, Dad in front and Mom snuggling him from behind. Watching them ride double back on the merry-go-round was a magical moment. It's nice when your parents are in love and not afraid to show it.

I enjoyed that night at the carnival with my family, and I'm glad Joyce was out of town. Had she been there, I might have missed the merry-go-round and the brass ring. I often wonder how many other brass rings my father captured for my mother, and none of us was around to see.

The carnival opened again the next day at 2:00 p.m., a nice arrangement since it was Sunday and families needed time for church and Sunday dinner. Steve Houchin and I decided to meet in front of the post office and hang out together. He was much more adventuresome than I, and we always had fun, with him usually taking the lead in determining what our fun would be. Because he was a cocky, well-built athlete, Steve was the kind of guy carnies try to rattle and goad into playing their games. A mouthy carny and cocky Steve getting crossways with one another would be interesting to watch. And in less than five minutes, the two combustibles sparked and flamed.

The first gaming booth we passed was one with three solid milk bottles stacked in a triangle, two on the bottom and one balanced on top. The object was simple: three throws for a quarter, knock down all three bottles, and win a prize. But there were a couple of catches, as there always are with carnival games. You had to knock down all three bottles with the first throw to win the big prize. Also, the bottles weren't regular milk bottles and looked weighted at the bottom. The balls were much softer than real softballs, more like big round pincushions, and their lack of heft was a definite disadvantage for the thrower.

Steve was one of our star pitchers in Little League and Pony League and later in high school. DeGraff had a tradition of fastball hurlers, and Steve Houchin could bring the heat as fast as any of them. So when the milk-bottle carny spotted him and challenged, "Hey, muscles, I'll bet you throw like a girl," I knew the action was about to begin.

Steve smirked. "How much?"

"Twenty-five cents, my muscled friend. That's one round quarter or two dimes and a nickel or five nickels or even twenty-five pennies, however you choose to pay. I accept all legal U.S. tender."

And Steve accepted all challenges. He pulled a carefully folded one-dollar bill out of his front pants pocket and slapped it on the counter.

"Give me my change up front. After my first throw, that big stuffed gorilla hanging up there will be mine."

The prizes displayed around the booth were separated according to the thrower's success. Knocking down all three bottles with the first throw won a large stuffed animal. If a second ball was needed, the prizes dropped down a notch to smaller stuffed animals and kewpie dolls. Using the third ball caused the prize to nosedive to a trinket or Hawaiian lei, the loser's consolation.

Steve had his eye on the big gorilla grinning down at him from the stuffed menagerie. His girlfriend was Roberta Dickerson, and I could tell he had already envisioned the kiss he'd receive from Roberta when he handed her the menacing miniature Kong. Steve was confident.

Unfortunately, confidence can turn its back and run rapidly from the premises. On Steve's first throw, ironically his best of the session, he smacked the bottom two bottles dead center, and although they wobbled enough to spill the bottle resting on top, they remained standing. He managed to knock down the right one with his second throw, but missed the remaining bottle with his third half-hearted pitch. No prize for Steve, not even a trinket or a lei.

"Set 'em up again," Steve demanded.

"Gladly, muscles," said the carny, smoothly scooping Steve's quarter into the canvas money pouch wrapped around his waist.

His second turn was as futile as the first with three mighty throws, one bottle still standing, and again not even a consolation prize. After the third quarter produced the same dismal results, he got more desperate with each squandered quarter. Steve was rattled, and the carny agitator knew he had Steve's number and his coins.

After going through three dollars, with two trinkets and a lei to show for his work, Steve turned to me.

"Give me a dollar!" No please, no thank you, but no way I wasn't going to hand one over—hard-earned or not. The look on Steve's face was one I'd seen only once before, and that was right after Jeremy Robinson from East Liberty drilled a Steve Little League fastball two hundred and fifty feet out of sight. Our three outfielders never found the ball, undoubtedly cowering somewhere within Lafe Funk's corn field planted well beyond the baseball diamond. When I trotted in from second base to calm Steve down, he gave me that look for the first time, and I hurried right back to my position. Steve struck out the next five batters, and we won the game nine to one.

There was to be no such happy outcome for this encounter. Eventually my three dollars went the way of Steve's three, and Mr. Gorilla continued to smile down on us. That was one dumb gorilla. Being propped up on Roberta Dickerson's bed would have been a much better fate than hanging around this portable gyp joint, but the big monkey didn't know any better, and his goofy grin remained fixed. We were broke.

Steve snarled, "Let's blow this place."

The carny sneered, "My pleasure, muscles."

I sniveled.

My day at the carnival was over, and I was out three dollars with no rides, no games, and no funnel cake. As we walked past the post office, Steve handed his fistful of cheap prizes to a couple of little girls coming into the carnival with their parents. They were happy.

We hiked down to the Bokenghelas Creek to skip rocks. Skipping flat rocks across the creek was our favorite way to relieve stress.

Steve missed the water with his first two throws.

My parents decided that I shouldn't hang around the carnival every day during its run. I protested a little, but since I lived under their roof and ate my daily meals for free, I acquiesced.

I'd chosen Saturday and Sunday, the first two days of the carnival, and the following Friday and Saturday, the last two, for my times to attend. But because Sunday with Steve was such a bust, my parents agreed to let me go back on Monday. They were usually fair that way.

I went alone and saw several of my friends but kept to myself. Since the milk bottle fiasco, I didn't want to spend much money but still treated myself to funnel cake and cotton candy. I was finishing the cotton candy when I stopped by a large tent in front of Hoke's Variety Store with a banner that read "Nature's Oddities." A barker caught me trying to peek inside the tent's open flap.

"Sonny, fifty cents lets you in to see something you'll never forget, something you never imagined. I promise you will be amazed and astounded."

"What will I see?" I was now curious, feeling in my pocket for two quarters.

"Inside this tent we have the smallest man in the world, and we have the fattest man in the world. Give me fifty cents, and you can watch them both for as long as you want."

I was hooked, but once inside I was disappointed. The fat man was sitting in a throne-like chair and talking to several people standing in front of him. A poster hanging prominently above his head displayed his picture and name, "Man Mountain Nelson." Someone in the crowd asked him to stand up and turn around, and I looked at the guy in disbelief. Man Mountain Nelson wasn't much bigger than Wimpy Knight or Turkey Thompson, DeGraff's heftiest citizens, and I could see either of them for free. Fattest man in the world! Heck, he was barely the fattest man in DeGraff.

I turned around, and on the other side of the tent was the smallest man. As advertised, he was small, and we had no one in DeGraff to equal his stature. He was the first little person I'd ever seen, and the name on his poster read, "Teenie Tiny Tim."

A ring of people were staring at him while he did his trick, walking in circles on broken glass scattered around him. After several steps on the glass, a kid who looked like one of the tangled rope kids from the Saturday setup dropped more bottles and broke them with quick whacks of a hammer. Teenie Tiny Tim then stomped on the new shards. Although the glass tramping seemed painless for him, his expression pained me. He glared at each one of us in the crowd while rhythmically jamming his stubby legs up and down on the glass. When he fixed his glare on me, for what seemed like an unbearable minute, I felt ashamed.

After his broken glass performance, Tim walked over to a dark corner of the tent and sat on the ground. He lit a cigarette, then brushed small pieces of glass from his callused feet. As he puffed in the shadows, the smoke surrounded his head and masked his face even more. Except for the slow movement of a lit hand to his mouth and away again, he stayed still. And as I watched him, I shared his humiliation. Before long I'd had enough and left the tent.

The barker called out to me as I stomped by, "Hey, sonny, how'd you like the act?"

I turned and glared at him, for what I hoped was an unbearable minute, then hurried home.

I Hope I'm Never Unglad

I rolled on the lawn yesterday.
I rolled and rolled and rolled.
When I finally stood,
I was itchy
and my face was red
and my clothes were stained with green.
But I didn't mind.

I'm glad it wasn't snow or mud,
that it was just an uncut lawn.
And I'm glad I was itchy and red and stained.
It's hard sometimes to be glad.
It's hard when you are looking for something
and you don't know where it is
or even what.

I'm glad there are lawns,
and I'm glad I like to roll on them.
I hope I never grow bored with it,
and I hope I'm never unglad.

XVII

House of Mirrors

Delivering the papers on Monday afternoon, while still reliving my carnival adventures and anticipating what was in store the next time, I made my routine stop at Bernie's house. He was stationed in his usual spot in the side yard. I'd already opened the paper to the comic section and was preparing to give Bernie his daily *Dick Tracy*, but he interrupted me as I was taking my first reading breath.

"Been to the carnival?"

"Yeah."

"Are you taking me?"

"I guess."

"When?"

"How about Friday?"

And that was that. Bernie and I had a date, and now all I had to do was break the news to Joyce. I had talked to her before about Bernie, and she seemed interested in meeting him, so I hoped she'd understand. I was going to joke with Bernie about how he'd be a third wheel, but after looking at him in his chair, I thought I'd better not. Heck, he was going to be an entire set!

When I explained the situation to Joyce, she was hesitant at first but warmed up to the idea with a little coaxing. After a few minutes, she even thought we'd enjoy ourselves. I suggested asking Steve and Roberta to join us, and Joyce agreed. All in all, the evening was shaping up to be a good one.

On Friday when I delivered the paper, Bernie was waiting in his side yard with a sweater doubled on his lap. Again, *Dick Tracy* dropped from the top of his priority list.

"Well, Bernie, you look ready for the carnival," I said, motioning toward the sweater.

"Mom thought I might get cold. What time we going?" He was anxious.

"How about six?"

"Good, now finish your route!" He was grinning like he always did when something out of the ordinary was about to happen. I finished my route in record time and got back to Bernie's house a little after 5:30 p.m. He looked even more ready, and I noticed several neatly folded dollar bills in his shirt pocket.

"Bernie, looks like you've got enough money to buy the carnival. Let me hold it for you. Somebody might pick your pocket, and you wouldn't even notice." I slipped the money from his pocket with a sleight of hand but bumped his chin for comic effect.

Bernie tried to give me a tough guy look. "That's five bucks, you crook, my mom counted it for me. I'm trusting you with it." I opened my billfold and nestled his money inside with mine. Then we were off.

I knew this was going to be a big evening for Bernie. He'd never been to anything like a carnival, and I was prepared to help him with sensory overload. I also had no idea what to expect, what he could or couldn't do. With Bernie impossible things somehow turned possible, but the carnival was going to present serious limitations for someone with his condition. In those days no one gave much thought to disability issues.

Bernie and I met Joyce by the railroad tracks on South Main in front of the big food concession tent. Joyce lived outside of town, and since I was still a few years shy of driving eligibility, her dad drove her into town for our dates. She was waiting for us with a sincere smile when I wheeled Bernie toward the tent, and she and Bernie hit it off immediately.

We went inside for something to eat, and Steve whistled to get our attention. Roberta acknowledged Joyce and me then went straight to Bernie to give him a quick hug. Bernie was having a great evening already with Roberta and Joyce fussing all over him, so Steve and I mocked being jealous. Bernie loved it.

Bernie never failed to fascinate me, and I enjoyed quietly studying him and his mannerisms. I am usually apprehensive in new situations, taking a while to relax and warm up to strangers. That wasn't the case with Bernie this evening. He immediately started to talk with the girls and to roll his head in a smooth, jerky, smooth, jerky figure-eight pattern. The head rolling was a common behavior when he got excited, and I suppose the movement looked odd to people who didn't know him. But I was used to it, and Joyce and Roberta didn't seem distracted.

Although I had to interpret for Bernie, my interjections didn't embarrass him. His sentences were strings of intelligible and unintelligible words, and I'd supply the hard-to-figure-out words in smooth transition, keeping Bernie from missing a beat. He did have a good sense of humor and was truly on in front of Joyce and Roberta, and I was proud to be his friend.

That was also the evening Bernie discovered funnel cake, and the two welcomed one another in style. Sitting in his wheelchair and looking like a throned Roman emperor being fed by two handmaidens, Bernie could barely chew fast enough to keep up with the pieces of sugar-sprinkled fried dough adorning his mouth from the graceful hands of Joyce and Roberta. By the time he finished, Bernie's mouth, cheeks, and chin were smudged white with powdered sugar.

"Hey, Bernie," I chided, "you look like your pal Flippo the Clown. You're a mess!" His attendants quickly began to wipe him clean. When Joyce licked her napkin and dabbed at his chin, Bernie almost swooned. Her gesture was probably the most sensuous act he'd ever experienced, and he feasted on it. I kidded Joyce later, but she didn't appreciate the insinuation, so I quickly dropped the subject.

By the time we finished eating it was almost 7:00 p.m., and Steve suggested we get moving. We went up and down each side of the carnival trying to decide what we wanted to do. As we walked, we each took a turn pushing Bernie, and he didn't seem like a fifth wheel at all. He was one of us for the evening, but that doesn't mean our adventure was without its challenges. The first awkward moment came as we passed the milk bottle booth, and the carny immediately recognized Steve.

"Is that you, muscles? How about another chance at Mr. Gorilla?" He spotted Roberta on Steve's arm. "Bet your girl could use something soft to cuddle up with at night. What you think, moon pie? Want muscles to win you something cuddly?"

I had to give Steve credit. He never said a word back to the jerk and didn't even look his way. Unfortunately, Roberta pulled away from him and walked over to the booth, spying the gorilla still smiling and hanging proudly.

"Oh, Steve, look how cute that gorilla is. I wish you'd win him for me."

I came to Steve's rescue. "Naw, that cheap stuff is for suckers. Let the suckers waste their money here. We've got better things to do."

Roberta seemed satisfied with my excuse, and Steve tossed me a thank you glance. Bernie, however, butted in with a comment about how cute the gorilla was and maybe we should take a chance. For once I was glad I was in control and quickly wheeled him away.

Our second awkward moment came at the Ferris wheel. By far the most impressive Ferris wheel I'd ever seen, the magnificently massive revolving circle of lights and gleaming steel dominated the intersection at the center of DeGraff's downtown streets and loomed over the four senior buildings—the Citizens Bank, the post office, Strayer's Department Store, and Morris Rexall Drugstore—stationed on each corner and standing guard for the other businesses. The buildings and Bernie looked up in envy. With no words spoken between us, Bernie and I both knew that the Ferris wheel was an adventure beyond our reach. We could conquer Thatcherville Hill but not this gyro-mountain.

The five of us looked at one another, waiting for someone to make a decision and admit the obvious. Steve finally broke the silence and suggested Roberta and Joyce ride with him while I stayed with Bernie. We agreed with silent nods of our heads, and the three of them climbed into a swinging car with Steve sitting in the middle. As they began to move forward, Bernie and I watched the slow ascent. I put my hands on his shoulders as our friends cranked higher and higher. The wheel gained speed, and they went round and round, waving each time they floated by.

"Looks like fun," Bernie spoke quietly. For the first time in my years of knowing him, Bernie Jones sounded defeated.

"Sure does, Bernie, sure does."

It did look like fun. I knew Joyce and I would eventually have our Ferris wheel ride. And I knew that Bernie would never have his, no matter how much we wanted it to be otherwise.

While they were circling, my brain was also circling and brooding about our carnival ride dilemma. Just before the three of them scrambled out of the car, jumped off the platform, and bounded down toward Bernie and me, I had a plan. Best of all, Mrs. Keenan was not around to challenge me on this one. The plan was pure genius!

"Hey, you guys," I blurted out as they hurried toward us, "remember the ride in front of Kinnan's Hardware, the one that looks like a bunch of giant teacups? That's a perfect ride for us to take Bernie on. That's a perfect ride!"

Joyce kissed me on one cheek while Roberta planted one on the other. Steve looked so pleased with my idea that I was afraid about his intentions and covered my mouth. He slapped me on the back.

"Let's go, Bernie," Steve announced while ushering Bernie through the crowd with the three of us parading close behind. "Let's go ride the mighty tea cups!"

I don't remember what the ride was actually called, but each circular rig on the horizontally revolving platform did resemble a big cup. The ride looked fun, safe, and Bernie proof, the exact combination we needed. Its mechanics were simple: the faster the speed of the entire platform, the more the individual cups swiveled round and round.

After we purchased our tickets and approached the platform with Bernie in tow, the ride operator looked hesitant, and I was afraid he was going to tell us Bernie couldn't get on. Steve didn't give him a chance.

"Hey, my good man, this guy has ridden every ride here, and this is the only one left for him to conquer. He decided he wanted to save the best for last." As Steve spun his line of bull, we began to unbuckle the wide leather strap keeping Bernie in his chair. Suddenly Bernie was free.

"Come on," Steve spun on, "let's get Bernie aboard before he decides this contraption is too slow for him."

Steve began to gather Bernie up from the right side, and I grabbed his left. As we gently lifted him, Bernie's eyes glided back and forth from me to Steve to me. He knew we were pulling a fast one and didn't want to give us away. This was something new for all of us, but we needed to act like we'd been performing our routine the whole evening. Bernie was doing his part by trying to look indifferent, but I knew Bernie, and I could tell his poor little heart was racing like a go-kart.

As we lifted him up and out and I saw the vacated wheelchair beneath him, I realized this was the first time I had ever seen Bernie out of his chair. The chair looked empty and small without him, and I was startled by the sight. The moment was an odd one for me, so I can hardly imagine how odd it must have been for Bernie. Being held aloft amidst a mass of strangers, Bernie was trusting his friend and his friend's friend with his life. In that moment he was completely vulnerable. Trust and friendship can go no deeper.

The man taking our tickets never had a chance to protest because we quickly swept Bernie into one of the big teacups and tightly squashed him into the middle of the four of us. The cup wasn't built for five, but we made it fit. As soon as the operator saw that we were loaded and ready, he pushed the lever full-throttle forward. We swung side to side to side, screaming and squealing and shrieking in laughter while, like an octopus, we held Bernie firmly in place with our combined eight hands. It was the ride of Bernie's life.

When we slowed to stop, Joyce yelled for the man to give us another ride and promised we'd pay after it was over. He slapped the lever forward, and again we tossed and turned and tethered onto Bernie for dear life.

After we finished the second time, we ladled Bernie out of the cup and poured him back into his chair. He was an ecstatic liquid quiver. Joyce re-buckled him while Roberta, feeling the air begin to chill, guided his wriggling arms and head into his sweater openings. I reached for my billfold and started toward the ticket booth to pay for our second ride, but the operator waved me off. "That one's on me. Just don't tell Big Red." I thanked him and promised to keep our secret.

We spent the rest of the evening going booth to booth and ride to ride. Earlier in the evening we had agreed not to leave Bernie alone, so sometimes Steve and Roberta would ride, and other times Joyce and I had our turn. Bernie never asked to ride on anything else and seemed content to watch. It's nice when once of something is enough.

We saved the Fun House for last. I had gone through the labyrinth earlier in the week to check out the features and make certain everything was safe and accessible for Bernie. The Fun House was actually just another big tent filled with unique displays and novelties arranged to scare kids and entertain adults.

Our favorite part was "The House of Mirrors." A series of mirrors distorted human bodies and faces into inhuman, grotesquely hilarious shapes and sizes. Bernie loved it, and we rolled him mirror to mirror and paused at each one so he could absorb the full comic effect. Steve, Roberta, and Joyce decided to stay for a while longer, but Bernie and I moved down to the next section of mirrors.

An incalculable number of mirrors were placed at various angles and heights, creating an unsettling illusion of multiplicity. Bernie and I were the only ones there. As we looked forward, we were surrounded by a myriad of our full-body images, much like a facetted prism repeats itself in symmetrically sunlit patterns along each wall.

We each studied our repeated selves—the older boy in his wheelchair and the younger boy behind him—and Bernie seemed to be seeing himself and us for the first time. He broke my heart when he finally spoke.

"We really are different, aren't we, Rickie?"

He looked so sad. I might have been able to fool one Bernie, but at that moment plural Bernies were too much for me to manage.

"We aren't that different, Bernie. You and I aren't that different. We really aren't."

My words sounded hollow. We were different, and the reflections of truth staring back at us did not lie no matter how hard I tried to.

The evening ended quietly. When Steve and Roberta left for his house, Joyce and I wheeled Bernie to her dad's car where he was patiently waiting by the railroad tracks. I gave her a quick hug and opened the door, reminding her that the next night, the last Saturday of the carnival, would be just for us. She smiled and leaned down to kiss Bernie on the forehead. Her hand lingered on his shoulder for a few seconds before she kissed his forehead again. As I began to close the car door, Bernie summed up his night with a simple, "Thanks," speaking perfectly for both of us.

After I pushed Bernie home and was opening the porch door for him, I slipped the five dollars back into his front shirt pocket. The move was my best sleight of hand, and he barely noticed. I stepped back and began to walk away, but then turned again to face Bernie, still sitting within the doorframe where I had wheeled him. "Sorry about the Ferris wheel, buddy."

Bernie almost looked me in the eye. "Oh, that's okay." For once he didn't sound convincing.

And for several months after, I wished I had done more.

The last evening of the carnival was for Joyce and me. We were finally together without family and friends and rode all the rides, except the Ferris wheel, at least once and some two or three times. We decided to save the Ferris wheel for our last romantic ride. The carnival didn't have that many rides, so I had more than enough money left for junk food and a couple games of chance.

I had managed to avoid the milk bottle booth, but toward the end of the evening when we were meandering, and I wasn't paying attention, we walked right up to it. The same smart aleck carny pitched me his taunts.

"Hey, little man, where's muscles this evening?" When he spied Joyce, he suddenly feigned suavity. "Ah, but I like what you traded him for. Nice taste, little man. Hey, apple dumpling, what can I do for you? Want to take a chance with me?"

I can fish all day and not have a fish take the bait as quickly as Joyce swallowed this guy's hook and line.

"Yes, I'd like that big gorilla up there. What do you think?" She looked right at me with those big brown eyes. "Can you win him for me?" My excuse for Steve had worked with Roberta, but I was out of luck with Joyce.

The mental image of Steve Houchin, a pure fire-balling pitcher extraordinaire, being turned into a flat-broke puddle of humiliation laughingly danced in front of the stacked milk bottles. This was shaping up to be the rotten end of a beautiful evening.

"Can you win him for me?" Joyce repeated, eyelids fluttering like twin hummingbirds. Being stuck between a rock and a hard place would have felt like a feather bed and down comforter compared to this vise grip.

"I can try, but don't get your hopes up," I whined lamely. "My arm kind of hurts today." Carny man shook his head and rolled his eyes like I was a loser already.

As I was reaching into my money pocket, mentally calculating how much this catastrophe was going to cost, a hand grabbed my shoulder and turned me around. I was facing Bill Haynes, my Little League baseball coach for three years. I had learned more about baseball from Bill Haynes than from any other coach. Bill knew baseball. He asked Joyce to excuse us for a minute and pulled me aside.

"Rickie, I traveled with a carnival one summer after high school. I helped out in a booth pretty much like this one and watched people throw their money away because they went at it all wrong. Listen carefully to me, and I'll explain how you win."

I always listened carefully to Coach Haynes, but this time I listened extra carefully. I had ears like an elephant.

"People make the mistake of throwing hard at the bottom two bottles and aiming right at the middle. That never works because the bottles are over-weighted from the middle down. Those soft balls aren't heavy enough to spill them. The secret"—my elephant ears grew longer and touched the pavement—"is to hit the two bottom bottles high on the rims. The ball has to hit those rims. Do that and all three will fall."

Bill patted me on the butt like he did one of his pitchers after a conference at the mound. If what he said was true, I believed I could do it. My arm wasn't very strong, causing my throws to arch slightly, but my aim was accurate. I felt certain I could hit the rims' sweet spot.

I winked at Joyce as I flipped mouth man my quarter. He placed the three cushioned softballs in front of me while pattering annoyingly, "I almost hate to take your money, little man, I almost hate to. But I will!"

My first throw was off the mark, hitting more of the right bottle's rim than the left's. The bottle on the right fell, as did the bottle it was holding up, but the left bottle only wobbled.

"Maybe you'll get that bottle with the next throw," Joyce encouraged, but I was already into my pocket for another quarter.

"I'm paying for another first throw. The young lady wants the big gorilla and nothing smaller."

"Good enough. I've got all night," annoying man answered back, scraping my quarter across the counter and into his canvas pouch.

"But I'd like to use the same ball again." I liked how it felt in my hand and wanted to stick with it. He retrieved the ball and flipped it back at me with an exaggerated underhanded motion.

I took a deep breath, stretched my arm, focused on the bottom bottles' upper rims, and made my pitch. The ball arched exactly toward the spot I was aiming for and thudded against the triangle. Like duckpins faced with a perfect pocket hit, the bottles gave up and fell down.

Joyce screamed.

Bill cheered.

I strutted.

Mouth man muted.

After our celebration, the carny reached up and unhooked the gorilla. He then tossed him over the counter at me.

"What's your name?" I asked. I thought I should know his name since we had done so much business together.

"Arnold," he answered.

"Well, Arnold, I'm Rickie, she's Joyce, and that guy is Bill." Then, handing Joyce the gorilla, I delivered my exit line. "Tell you what, Joyce, I think we should name this big ape Arnold." We peacocked away.

As I turned around to give the real Arnold one last look, he was already hanging another stuffed gorilla on the vacated hook. He winked at me and pointed to a big box stuffed with gorillas. Even when you win, carnies don't lose.

The time was close to 10:00 p.m., the hour Joyce was to meet her dad, so we headed to the Ferris wheel for our last ride. This was my first time to ride it, and I had looked forward to the thrill all week. Only one other couple was on the wheel when the operator helped us into the car.

We started slowly then gained speed. I loved the sensation as we circled up and down, down and up while feeling the warmth of Joyce snuggled closely beside me. Some of life's best moments are the innocent ones, and if you're lucky enough, you realize how special they are before they pass. I was sorry that Bernie would never experience his moment. But in his world of vicariousness, this was just one more episode he'd have to live through me. We all have a purpose.

After several revolutions, we slowed to a stop as our car reached the very top, and I looked down at the operator waving up to us. Everything was still and quiet, and as I slowly turned my head, I could see my whole world encircling me. I saw all of DeGraff dressed up in nighttime lights, and my hometown looked so big; and my hometown looked so small. And I felt so big; and I felt so small. I could not imagine being anywhere else in the world, and I was glad to call DeGraff my home.

In the distance I saw the flat spreading roofs of the box factory, shut down for the evening so that second-shift workers could enjoy the carnival with their families. Bernie's house was faintly visible and cuddled near the box factory, but kept from intimacy by two strands of railroad track stitched between them. I knew Bernie was asleep somewhere within that small square of a child's block. I wondered if he was safely still within his bed sheets or if his body continued to twitch and contort and fight the sheets even at rest. I wondered if life ever paused and quieted for him and his body. I wondered if he dreamed wheel-less dreams and longed for walking worlds in make-believe. I wondered…

Joyce nudged me back to her, breaking my trance. And then we kissed.

The whole town seemed empty the next morning when Dad drove us to church. The carnival had packed up and pulled out during the middle of the night. Big Red skipped out without paying me for his week of papers, the first time I'd ever been stiffed by a customer. P.T. Barnum was right, and I was the sucker for that day.

After church I decided to walk home, and in front of the post office I found a ticket for one of the rides. I picked it up and saved it for Joyce's scrapbook.

CARNIVAL COMING TO TOWN!

CARNIVAL COMING TO TOWN!

CARNIVAL COMING TO TOWN!

The next summer the same carnival came back to DeGraff. Jeff and Mike Bodenmiller again hammered signs around town, and during the setup day I saw the two rope-wrangling boys. They now looked like official roustabouts as they carried a tamed, perfectly wound rope easily between them. Big Red parked his Airstream in the same spot by Stayrook's Auto Sales. As I pedaled my bike to deliver Andy's paper, Big Red saw me and called out, "Hey, fella, is that the local paper you're carrying?"

I was ready for him.

"Yes, Big Red, it is, and it's the same paper you didn't pay me for last summer. Remember the deal we had? If you want a paper this week, I need paid in advance and also paid for last year. That will cost you sixty cents."

Although he turned an even darker crimson, I'm certain he didn't remember me at all. Who knows how many times Big Red had scammed little kids out of their paper money? I was just one paperboy in a ream of newspapers throughout his travelogue of small towns. He shook his head and laughed.

"You got me, fella, you got me dead to rights." He crammed his fat red hand into the front pocket of his overalls, waded around, pulled out a coin, and flipped it to me. It was a silver dollar.

"You carried my debt for a whole year. Will that cover it and the paper for this week?"

For some reason I bit the coin the same way I had seen Gabby Hayes do a dozen times in movie westerns. It tasted horrible, and I wondered what else Big Red stashed away in his pockets. I wasn't even certain why I was biting the silver dollar, but I bit it a second time just for effect. No wonder Gabby was toothless!

"Yeah, Big Red, this will cover it. I like doing business with you."

Big Red smiled, then he turned and went into his trailer. I still have the silver dollar.

The carnival was just as much fun as the summer before, only this time I shared the rides with Marilyy Herndon. Joyce had decided she liked older men who could drive. Or maybe her dad just got tired of hauling her around. Who can figure women out?

On the first day of the carnival I walked by the tent of "Nature's Oddities," and the same barker as before called out to me.

"Sonny, fifty cents lets you in to see something you'll never forget, something you never imagined. I promise you will be amazed and astounded."

"And what will I see that's so amazing?" I asked, already knowing the answer.

"You will see Pretzel Man, who can twist his body into any shape, and you will see Lady Nellie, the fattest bearded woman in the world."

I was shocked. "What happened to Tim and Man Mountain Nelson?"

"Well, Teenie Tiny married a schoolmarm in Idaho and quit the show, and Man Mountain went on a diet, so Big Red fired him."

Curious, I paid the man and went inside the tent. Pretzel Man was a major disappointment. Charles Tamplin, who delivered newspapers with me, was more double-jointed than Pretzel Man and had more disjointed moves than this guy ever dreamed of.

And as I peered closely at Lady Nellie, she looked a whole lot like Man Mountain Nelson, only with a beard. I figured she might be Man Mountain's sister or maybe Man Mountain himself in disguise. Who knew? Although P.T. Barnum's words were again echoing through my head, I sure hated to think a carnival would intentionally swindle a kid.

XVIII

The Warmth of a New Morning

The two most uncertain periods in my life happened within months of one another. I graduated from high school in June, and in September I began school all over again as a freshman at Ohio State University. I was sad at my graduation party and seemed to be the only one not having fun. My family had me pose for dozens of pictures in my red cap and gown, and I felt like a butterfly ready to be released from its ruddy cocoon, left on its own to flutter. Except I wanted to be re-cocooned. I'd been successful in high school, and everyone had big expectations for me as a college student, but I liked my life in DeGraff just the way it was.

Leaving my hometown would not be easy. Columbus was imposing, Ohio State immense, and I was assigned to a freshmen dormitory housing almost as many students as DeGraff had citizens. In DeGraff I had a name; at Ohio State I'd be a fraction of a multi-digit number.

I also had difficult good-byes to make. Not only was I leaving my hometown, I was letting go of my paper route and nine years of loyal customers. And I was abandoning Bernie.

Because I was his older brother, Jeff often received my discarded hand-me-downs grudgingly: clothes, shoes, school supplies, baseball gloves, and even a despondent girlfriend. When I gave him my paper route, he finally appreciated something I had outgrown.

A Saturday in early September was to be my last official contact with my customers. The next day I was leaving for Ohio State. I figured after I told my customers good-bye when collecting for the paper, seeing them again later in the day would be difficult, so I asked Jeff to make the paper deliveries for Saturday afternoon—except for three special deliveries I wanted to make myself.

Since I didn't finish the collections until several hours past my normal time and late into the afternoon, I was glad I'd asked Jeff to deliver the papers. The stops at each house took longer than usual and each had a special significance. My first customer, Janet Hall, had a freshly baked apple dumpling for me, my usual Christmas treat, and she asked me to stay and enjoy it while we talked. She was a genuine listener, and I was with her for half an hour.

Andy Stayrook was a quiet man who seldom had much to say, but we talked for several minutes. He told me how he had planned to go to college but never made it out of DeGraff. Marriage, children, and work took priority. I asked if he had any regrets, and he answered he didn't, but he emphasized he didn't want me to have any regrets either and made me promise I'd study hard and graduate.

Bernie wasn't in the side yard when I stopped to collect, and that was unusual. His dad told me Bernie wasn't feeling well. When he paid me for the paper, Frank Jones gave me a twenty-five-cent tip, and that was also unusual.

Miss Lizzie's money was under the front doormat, her regular hiding place when she didn't want to come to the door, so I didn't see her. Since she was on my special delivery list, I knew I'd see her later in the day.

Mrs. Hostetler apologized for not having any homemade cookies, but when I saw a plate covered with aluminum foil on the front porch table, I figured something was up. She handed me the plate and took a step back, smiling. The plate felt heavy, and when I removed the foil, I found ten fifty-cent pieces spread out like cookies. That got to me, and Mrs. Hostetler could see the emotion on my face. Emotional herself, she said college guys always needed extra spending money. She kissed me on the cheek, turned, and walked back to the front door, standing for a couple of seconds before waving and going inside.

The final bike ride up and down Thatcherville Hill was difficult. Since the day I had taken Bernie with me to collect, I felt especially close to my Thatcherville customers. Also, a couple of years before, Lady had chased a squirrel across the road and run right in front of a car traveling up the hill. The car hit Lady's backside and spun her around into another car driving downhill that also struck her. I was certain she'd been killed, but when I ran up to her, disregarding traffic myself, her eyes were open and she was breathing.

Lula Taylor saw the accident from her front porch and called the local vet, Dr. Verbsky. In those wonderful days of house calls, he was there in less than five minutes. The two of us carefully lifted Lady onto his backseat for her ride to the veterinary clinic, and she spent a month there while Dr. Verbsky nursed her back to health. Lady had two broken hips and limped for the rest of her life, but she still followed me on the route, though slower and less squirrel aware. She seemed to sense that this Saturday was her final time as well for the paper route and Thatcherville. For reasons only a dog can explain, she never followed Jeff. I think it was because he couldn't whistle.

I collected a lot of gifts and encouragement that Saturday. Fortunately, I had a wide-wire basket on the front of my bike and a wide-open mind grateful for small-town advice. Jake Long gave me a thesaurus from his days as a student at Ohio State; Mrs. Frantz collected a small bag of good luck buckeyes; Mrs. Keenan put together a cardboard box of first aid materials, "Since your mom will not be around to take care of you"; Bill Shoemaker handed me a pocket compass because, "Ohio State is so dadgum big." My basket was overflowing.

And God bless Sis Knight. Sis, a numismatist who saw budding numismatic qualities in me, was sitting on his porch waiting for my arrival. In a grand gesture he paid me for the paper with one penny, a 1931S worth about $18.00. He said he'd found the penny a few days earlier in some change he'd received from Auggie Leagre at the post office, but I didn't believe him. I think he had planned my surprise for some time. He was pretty pleased with himself, and we admired the penny for several minutes before I moved on.

But of all the gifts I received on my day of good-byes and good wishes, none equaled the heartfelt practicality of what Mrs. Harshbarger gave me. The Harshbargers lived atop Harshbarger Hill, the steepest climb in DeGraff. Six days a week standing upright and pumping hard, I pedaled up the hill to deliver their paper. Mr. and Mrs. Harshbarger were my only customers out that direction from town, over half a mile both ways from the rest of my route, but because they were such a sweet elderly couple, I didn't mind. I made only one thin dime weekly for my efforts, but the pay didn't matter. Because I was lucky to have a paper route, I thought of it as my *pro bono* contribution to the profession.

Mr. Harshbarger was stooped outside a storage shed sharpening the blades on his lawnmower. The mower was an old-fashioned push kind with an oblong set of rotating circular blades. Because he was a man well into his seventies who cut an acre of grass weekly by pushing a truly self-propelled lawnmower, I never complained about my bike rides up his hill. His generation already thought my generation was soft, and I didn't want to give him any further proof.

"Your lawn looks great, Mr. Harshbarger. This summer's rains have kept you busy, but you always seem to be a step ahead of the grass." He was a tall, lanky man who had mastered the art of looking over his glasses at you while continuing to do whatever he was doing.

"Yep, I've got to keep ahead of it. Grass never sleeps, you know, except for the big winter nap. If this yard ever gets ahead of me, I'm a dead man. Mrs. Harshbarger would kill me."

I laughed. "But if she killed you, Mr. Harshbarger, she'd have to mow all this by herself!"

He chuckled back. "Please tell her that for me. I'm not certain she's considered the consequences."

Digging into his front pocket for change and then counting it out to me coin by coin, he again peered over his glasses. "Go on into the kitchen through the side porch door, young man. The missus has something for you."

When I reached the porch and opened the door, he shouted over to me, "And good luck in college."

Mrs. Harshbarger was sitting at the kitchen table, a cup of tea in front of her. The tea bag on the saucer looked almost dried out, and I had the feeling she'd been sitting for some time waiting for me. She probably had. The Harshbarger house was toward the end of my route, and I was running late.

"Good afternoon, Mrs. Harshbarger. How you doing today?"

She smiled the kind of soft smile grandmothers worldwide have perfected and patented. "I'm just fine today, Rickie, just fine today. You're late."

"Yes, ma'am." I apologized for courtesy, even though I'd done nothing wrong. "Yes, ma'am, I am late today. This is my last day, you know."

Her soft eyes continued to look at me like she was seeing me for the first time. Or maybe she knew this might be the last.

"I have watched you mature over these past years. I remember the day you started your route. You were such a little guy, and Mr. Harshbarger was sure you wouldn't last, thought maybe our hill would make you quit delivering the paper." Softly, she continued to look at me. "But I told Mr. Harshbarger you'd make it, that you would not quit on us. And I was right. Even now you aren't really quitting. You are simply setting this hill aside for bigger ones to climb."

I wanted to say something back to her, something meaningful, but I could tell she had more to say, more she'd been thinking about while waiting. "When Mr. Harshbarger and I were married, Mother wanted to give me a special gift, a useful gift just for me. Daddy gave us a pregnant sow. He knew the sow would be useful, and she was. You know, we had offspring of that sow every Easter and Christmas family dinner for almost fifty years. Isn't that a remarkable thing?"

I smiled yes to her.

"Mother wanted me to have something useful as well, something I'd appreciate every day. I think she also wanted me to have something to remind me of her every day." She paused, soft eyes still holding me. "You know what she gave me?"

I smiled no.

"Mother told me that when she was a little girl, she disliked getting out of bed early in the morning. She didn't like the early morning because the first thing she felt was the cold floor on her bare feet. 'Terrible way to start a day,' she'd always say. So her mother, my grandmother, taught Mother how to make a rug from rags. Mother made herself a small rug out of rags and laid the rug on the hardwood floor beside her bed. Every morning for the rest of her life, the rag rug was the first thing to touch Mother's feet."

Mrs. Harshbarger paused and softly nibbled her lower lip. "When Mr. Harshbarger and I married, Mother gave me a rag rug she'd made herself. And every day of my married life, when I get out of bed, the first thing I feel is her rug against my feet."

I wanted to say something but remained silent.

Mrs. Harshbarger's soft hands reached below the table and gently lifted a brown Fuson's IGA grocery sack she'd been cradling on her lap. She placed the sack on the table and slowly slid it toward me.

"I've made something for you. Wherever you go, wherever your life takes you, I want your feet to touch the warmth of a new morning, like my feet have for so many years. I am giving you the beginning of a warm day."

I wanted to say something, but now I didn't have the words. I reached across the table and touched her soft, wrinkled cheek. It was warm. "Thank you, Mrs. Harshbarger," was all I could manage.

The rag rug Mrs. Harshbarger made for me was the first thing I unpacked at Ohio State. I unfurled it beside my bed on the dormitory's sterile linoleum floor. And every day of my undergraduate life, no matter how cold it was, that rug was my warmth of a new morning.

XIX

Sometimes Good-bye
Does Mean Good-bye

After collecting from my customers for the final time, I biked home slowly to carefully protect the generous bounty I'd gathered. I carried the items upstairs and spread them on my bed to show my parents that evening. I then went downstairs and waited on the front porch for Jeff to return from delivering the papers on his route. His route? I felt like a stranger in my own land.

As Jeff turned his bike into our driveway, I hurried over to ask him for the newspapers I wanted to deliver myself. He handed me *The Belle-fontaine Examiner* canvas bag with three folded papers inside. I looped the bag over my shoulder as I had done a couple of thousand times before and climbed aboard my bike for the last deliveries. I called to Lady, who was flopped down in the grass beside our garage, and she looked up, surprised to see me ready to ride again. Tail wagging, she arose gingerly, arthritic hips slowing her, but managed to prance closely behind as I pedaled down Mill Street and glided onto Race Street.

Race Street slopes slightly downhill, and I could coast a good distance. On my right was Ernie's pasture field, meadow-green and dissected by the Bokenghelas, with the bridge at the bottom of the hill trying to stitch the incision. I caught a quick glimpse of the roof of our house and visualized Mom in the kitchen and Dad in his easy chair, heavy eyed and pretending to read *The Examiner.* It's nice to know everything is in place even though you will soon be out of yours. I pedaled a couple of hundred more yards before turning onto Boggs Street to begin the first of my final deliveries.

Fern Burdette's house stood empty since her death five years before. After a nephew and his wife arrived from California to loot all they wanted of Fern's possessions, an auction was held to sell the rest. Everything sold but the house itself, and that surprised me because I thought her house was perfect. But people said it needed too much fixing and wasn't worth the repair expenses. Fern would have spit.

I parked my bike on the sidewalk and walked to the porch. Lady was already there curiously sniffing the corner of the porch where Fern's Duke had rested. Lady circled twice and then sat, paws crossed prayer-like. I watched her and figured she might understand our purpose.

I opened the screen door, unfolded the paper, and carefully rested it against the locked front door, headlines facing up and out. I remembered the words of Fern's first boss, and the advice he'd given her when she was an apprentice journalist.

"Fern, never hide the news from your readers. Keep it right in front of them."

When I closed the screen door, the headlines were boldly visible just the way Fern liked them. As I got back onto my bike and called for Lady, I smiled and looked skyward.

I pedaled past the box factory and bounced over the railroad tracks. Bernie was sitting in his side yard and watching my direction, but he seemed to be looking past me.

"Hey, Bernie," I yelled, "I'm stopping at Miss Lizzie's. You want me to wheel you over?" Still managing not to look at me, his head wobbled a no.

"Okay, buddy, I'll be right back."

When I stopped at Miss Lizzie's, I saw to my complete amazement that she was sitting on the porch, self exiled from the safety of her house. Beside her chair were two creaseless, foiled pumpkin breads. I dismounted my bike and waved a hello, but I could see she was extremely uncomfortable.

"Great day to be outside, isn't it, Miss Lizzie?"

"I suppose," she answered unconvincingly.

Miss Lizzie looked out of place even in her place—on the porch of the house that had served as home for over half a century.

"I figured when I saw your little brother go by earlier, without leaving me my paper, that you might deliver it yourself. I was hoping you would."

Miss Lizzie leaned down and carefully lifted both loaves up and onto her lap.

"Your brother looks nice. Your parents are doing a good job raising you boys."

"Thanks, Miss Lizzie. Yeah, Jeff's okay, and he'll be a decent replacement. I think you'll like him."

As she stood, I noticed how sad she looked, and I felt sad with her. She handed me the treasured loaves, grazing my hand twice. Then very simply and very gently, she brushed her hand through my hair and whispered, "When you find your love, keep her. And, my friend, be safe. The world is a dangerous place. Please be safe." With that she scurried into her house and closed the door.

I carefully set the loaves in the basket and climbed onto my bike, all the while looking back at Miss Lizzie's front door. I made a U-turn and coasted back to Bernie's, parking on the grass a few feet from him. He still wouldn't look at me, and I tried to ignore the discomfort for both of us.

"Bernie, are you feeling better? You weren't outside when I collected this morning. Your dad told me you weren't feeling so hot."

He answered but didn't perk up. "Yeah, I'm okay. I'm just tired."

Neither of us spoke, and Lady nuzzled at the foot of his chair. He tried to ignore her as well but couldn't resist her persistence.

Bernie finally broke the silence while looking down at Lady instead of up at me. "Think Lady will miss me?"

"Of course she will, Bernie, we'll both miss you."

I had dreaded this moment for months. Back in the early spring, I told Bernie about my plans for college and that I was passing the paper route down to my brother. I explained all of the reasons and answered all of his questions, but he didn't understand then either.

He was upset, and we didn't talk about it again. But the day we'd both avoided was here.

"Mom's going to help me with *Dick Tracy*," he said as flatly as he could manage, eyes still cast downward and fixed on Lady. That was Bernie, out-of-the-blue Bernie.

"What?" I asked, knowing what he had said but asking anyway. "What did you say?"

"Mom's going to help me read *Dick Tracy*. She said she'd fold the paper for me." He was making his point.

"Bernie, I told you my brother Jeff will read *Dick Tracy* to you just like I always have. Jeff will read to you."

I watched him carefully, waiting for him to give me a sign, any sign of forgiving me for leaving. It never came, and this time our silence was even longer and more excruciating. Then Bernie, the one between us who had trouble speaking, broke the silence again.

"It won't be the same, Rickie. It won't be the same."

"I know, Bernie. I know it won't."

He finally looked up at me. And as I looked back at him, I knew I had made a terrible mistake the past several months. I had not been honest with Bernie, and I was the one person, maybe the only person, he could count on to be honest with him. I'd been acting like everything would remain the same for Bernie, like things wouldn't change at all. I figured I was the one changing, not him. I was the one whose whole life was turning topsy-turvy, upside down, and 180 degrees around. But that wasn't true, and I was wrong. I was not the only one changing. Bernie's life was changing while remaining exactly the same.

For a fraction of a second, as I looked into his eyes, I saw the world as Bernie saw it, and the view broke my heart. His world was one long tunnel of waiting.

I placed the folded newspaper on his lap and, leaning forward, gently hugged his neck. I felt his arms trying to reach around me, but they couldn't manage it. It didn't matter. We both felt his hug.

"See you, Bernie."

"Promise?"

"Promise."

"See you, Rickie, my boy."

I put my hands on his shoulders and looked into his eyes one more time. Then I quickly turned, got on my bike, and rode away.

On the ride home I glanced again at the pasture field I had treasured for so many years. Shadows from several trees, especially the trees by the creek, were stretching out and reaching up the hill toward our house. I hurried home, not wanting to be late and miss a minute.

The next day I left for college. After driving away from our house, I cruised around the school grounds a couple of times, headed downtown, circled back to see Bernie's house, rode up and down Thatcherville Hill, went back downtown, and then drove through Greenwood Cemetery before finally speeding beyond the city limits sign. I was satisfied I had seen it all.

The following year my dad was offered a teaching position at Kent State University, and my family moved to Kent, Ohio. I did return to DeGraff for a few class reunions, weddings, and funerals, but each time I went back I felt more like my hometown's friend and less like a relative. Looking back now I feel certain, somehow, that I must have realized I was formally leaving DeGraff behind the day I said my good-byes and left for college. And in the way people said their good-byes back to me, I should have known it was official.

Life is a shedding away, and small towns are used to watching their children spread their wings and leave the nest. Sometimes good-bye does mean good-bye.

AND I WAS GONE

I saw myself
in your eyes,
and I was sorry
because you looked
so lonely.
But then you blinked
and I was gone.

XX

Promises

Soon after we were married, Sherée asked me to make two promises. First, she made me promise I would take her to DeGraff. Because I talked so much about DeGraff and my friends, she felt she already knew most of them informally and deserved to be formally introduced. Her second request was more challenging. Afraid I would begin to forget the stories I repeated so often, she made me promise to write about life in DeGraff. I promised to do both.

I'd also made a promise to an old friend many years ago. I promised Bernie Jones I would see him again. Technically, I had kept the promise, but only technically. I did see Bernie once again after the day I delivered his paper for the final time.

Over Christmas break of my freshman year at Ohio State, Mrs. Webb, the Methodist minister's wife, gathered several of us to go caroling one snowflaked evening a few days before Christmas. We sang around town, stopping primarily at the homes of elderly Methodist Church members. As we caroled on the porch of Skinner Hittepole's Grandma Spain, we were only a few blocks from Bernie's house, and I asked if we could go there and sing for him. Walking down Boggs Street toward Bernie's instead of riding my bike felt strange.

When we arrived at Bernie's and began to sing "Silent Night," the porch light came on, and Mrs. Jones wheeled him through the front door. He spotted me immediately within the chorus—Bernie's ability to focus his eyes always amazed me—and he grinned his silly grin while flapping both arms and kicking his legs in the air. The way he mouthed "Rickie, my boy" over and over and over again icicled through my heart. After we finished "Silent Night" and before "The First Noel," I pulled away from the semi-circle of singers and walked quickly to him.

I took one of his waving hands in mine and held it tightly against my thick coat. I felt awkward. I was ashamed for feeling awkward and didn't know why I was so uncomfortable, but time and distance change many things. Even though I'd been gone for only a few months, my life in DeGraff now seemed like someone else's life from a lifetime ago. But Bernie didn't seem to notice, and he never moved his eyes away from me.

I was wearing a red Santa Claus cap with a small bell attached to the bottom of the cone-shaped tassel sloping down from the top. I removed the cap and placed it on Bernie's head. He liked that and laughed while my friends applauded. Leaning down, I wished Bernie a Merry Christmas and grabbed his hand for a final time. He said something to me, but I couldn't understand his words and didn't ask him to repeat them.

Then I let him go.

His hand remained upright and writhing, outstretched toward me as I hurried back into the chorus. When we finished our caroling and began to walk away, I turned. He looked sadappy. I felt sad.

I heard the bell on the Santa cap jangle in sporadic rhythms as we passed the box factory. And I will swear I could hear it still, an hour later, as I walked alone on Mill Street.

Six years later, after graduating from college and completing my second year of teaching, I returned to DeGraff to attend Skinner Hittepole's wedding. I drove to Bernie's house after the ceremony. I was stunned as I passed over the railroad tracks. His house was gone, replaced by an additional box factory parking lot that spread to within a few feet of Miss Lizzie's house.

I could not believe my eyes as I glared at the vast expanse of black-top and tried to remember where Bernie sat in his side yard, waiting patiently for me to deliver the paper and read *Dick Tracy*. Bernie and his house were gone, and I was angry for not keeping my promise.

I tentatively knocked on Miss Lizzie's door. Although I heard a shuffling inside and thought I saw the slight movement of a front window curtain, she didn't answer. I only knocked once.

I then drove to Taylor's Restaurant, figuring someone there might be able to tell me about Bernie. Sam Hamsher, now using a cane and looking much older than I remembered, outlined the sketchy details. Bernie's parents had both died a couple of years before, and he'd been taken in by a relative of his mother's living somewhere in northwestern Ohio. That's all Sam knew, and no one in Taylor's Restaurant or the post office or Kinnan's Hardware could tell me anything more, not even the relative's name or the city they lived in. And that was it for Bernie and me.

Over the years I heard nothing more about Bernie Jones until the night my mother called to tell me Jinny Knief had located him. He was now living in a nursing home in Lakeview. My pilgrimage back to Ohio had even more meaning. I was going home to celebrate my cousin's wedding, and I was going home to keep a promise.

XXI

A Promise Finally Kept

My cousin's wedding was perfect. Coming home to relatives you grew up with, after years of geographic separation, is nostalgia in its purest form. Conversations never lag because each story, embellished by time, is better than the one before it. I loved being with my family, and I cherished the echoes of reminiscence.

After a big Sunday morning breakfast—my Aunt Sally is famous for her cornucopian breakfasts—I began my journey to the Heartland Nursing Home. Heartland was the same nursing home my Granddad Niece had been admitted to many years before during the final week of his life.

Granddad was admitted for only three hours before he called my dad and demanded to be taken home. Dad complied with his wishes and cancelled the paperwork admitting his father. I'm fairly certain my grandfather remains the least tenured resident in Heartland Nursing Home history.

He had terminal cancer, and he did not want to die in a strange bed in a strange room in a strange place surrounded by strangers. Granddad wanted to die in the comfort of his own home, and five days later he did. The terminally ill usually know what is best for them, while the rest of us spend their precious remaining hours guessing around it.

As I drove to the nursing home and thought about Bernie, I didn't know what I was feeling. I was a cocktail mix of nervous, anxious, curious, and a twist of panic. I wondered what I was doing, why I hadn't done it sooner, and how I would react when I saw Bernie. As I got closer to Lakeview, I tried not to think at all. But all I did was think and, consequently, I didn't know what I was feeling.

After I pulled into the paved lot at Heartland, I sat in the car to gather my scattering thoughts before going inside. Looking through the car window, I watched three men in wheelchairs, two on the front porch and one in the side lawn. I squinted my eyes trying to telescope my vision and get a better look at them. For all I knew any of the three could have been Bernie, especially the one in the side yard. When I got out of the car and walked past them, I made a point of greeting each one personally. They were friendly and pleased to be acknowledged, but none was Bernie. They looked well cared for, and I felt satisfied they'd never be left outside in a thunderstorm.

I entered the front doors into the lobby area, and a receptionist directed me to the nurses' station. The hallway to the station was narrowed by elderly residents, some in wheelchairs, others on four-legged walkers, and a few leaning crookedly against the wall. Intravenous apparatuses, institutional gowns and slippers, and portable oxygen appeared to be the day's fashion accessories. As I inched by, I tried to smile at the residents, not merely out of a sense of friendliness but to peruse them carefully. I wanted to see if I could detect a semblance of the Bernie Jones I used to know. Although their faces peered back with shades of hopeful recognition, Bernie was not among them.

The nurses' station was at the end of the hallway and served as a check-in point for visitors and a way station for patients shuffling between rooms. Another chorus of curious faces greeted me. I asked one of the nurses about Bernie, and she said he was in room 102 and pointed around the corner. As I turned ninety degrees and entered a different corridor, I saw 102 on a slightly opened door. Bernie's name was permanently attached below the number. Sucking down a deep breath, I took several nervous steps forward and crossed the threshold into Bernie's world once again.

Bernie was lying on the bed, his arms and legs still jerking unwittingly although not as dramatically as I thought I remembered from years ago. His wheelchair sat vacant in a corner. I had seen him out of his chair only once before, when Steve Houchin and I lifted him onto the carnival ride, but I had never seen him prone. He was watching NASCAR racing on a small color television sitting on a clothes dresser pressed against the wall in front of him. He hadn't noticed I'd come into his room, allowing me to glance around.

Several NASCAR posters dominated the walls, and most were pictures of one driver, Jeff Gordon, and his brightly colored #24 DuPont race car. The room was humble and tidy, efficient and pasteurized. As I glanced toward Bernie again, his head yanked toward his visitor. Our eyes met, and I could see an uncertain recognition on his face. I moved toward him.

"Hey, Bernie, it's Rick Niece, your paperboy from DeGraff." I quickly rephrased my greeting. "Bernie, it's Rickie Niece."

Each time I think back to that moment, the instant he recognized me and knew for certain who I was, I feel a groundswell of uninhibited emotion. I have never seen such an instantaneous expression of shock and delight. The look filled his face, spilled onto the pillow, and flooded over the bed.

"Rickie?"

"Rickie, my boy?"

"Rickie, my boy!"

I tried to hug him, but we couldn't manage a real hug. I felt his arms struggle for my back, and that, once again, was enough.

"So, Bernie, are the nurses around here as pretty as Sparkle Plenty or Rita?"

Bernie laughed, and I immediately noticed he didn't have any teeth. I had prepared myself for how his crusty, yellowed teeth would look all these years later, but I hadn't prepared myself for Bernie having only bare, shiny gums for his smile. His hair was cut short and brushed up, and I reached out to stroke my hand across his head.

"Bernie Jones, is that a"—I paused for dramatic effect—"is that a flattop you're sporting? I thought we hated Flattop Jr."

Another throaty laugh emerged from Bernie. "Nope, no flattop, just a buzz."

A nurse came into the room and muted the television while leaving the video on. She asked if we were okay, and I told her we were terrific.

"So, Bernie, you like NASCAR?" I asked, motioning toward the screen and poster-adorned walls.

"Oh, yeah."

Looking at his posters, I smiled and gave a thumbs-up. "I take it you like number twenty-four."

"Oh, yeah."

I told Bernie that Sherée and I had recently gone to a NASCAR race in Daytona. I'd never been a fan of NASCAR before meeting Sherée and didn't fully comprehend the concept of grown men driving around in circles. But I married into a family of big fans, especially Sherée and her dad, and was now a fan myself. Sherée's favorite driver was also Jeff Gordon, and when I told Bernie he shared a favorite with my wife, he flashed another shiny-gummed grin.

"How much are tickets?" he asked.

When I told him our tickets were $150 apiece, Bernie's eyes got round like hubcaps, and he uttered a "Wow!" that had at least five syllables. Looking at him lying there in his scantily furnished room, I was suddenly embarrassed about the extravagance of $300 for a car race. I didn't dare mention the $8.00 hot dogs or $4.50 soft drinks.

We then began a real conversation, sharing memories we had both kept treasured and safely guarded. Bernie's speech and unique sentence rhythms hadn't improved, and I struggled at first but eventually understood most of what he said. I was proud of us both. Bernie asked where I lived, and I told him I had flown to Ohio from Arkansas. He questioned why I had come so far to Ohio, and without hesitation I gave him the only answer necessary.

"Bernie, you're the reason I came back home."

He was quiet for a moment, his eyes darting back and forth and up and down me. After all these years, his eyes were still the only muscles he could fully control, and at that moment his control was masterful.

"You came to see me?"

"I sure did, Bernie, I sure did."

Later, when I was able to talk to the nursing home administrator, I learned why he was so grateful for company: Bernie had few visitors. Besides an occasional visit from a couple of relatives, his only regular visitor was a social worker from Bellefontaine, and her stay was clinically routine. She also explained that Bernie had become very difficult to handle, earning himself quite an unfavorable reputation among several nursing homes throughout the region. When something or someone upset him, and I was warned he was easily upset, he'd defiantly demand to be checked out and placed somewhere else. Bernie had been through a number of institutions, but Heartland seemed to be working out for now, his second time around. She assured me that Bernie and the nurses at Heartland were finally growing tolerant of one another, and I felt better about his situation.

The longer Bernie and I talked, the more comfortable we became, and the memories flowed fast and easy. Each time I brought up a topic like the carnival or Thatcherville Hill or our game of horseshoes, he'd light up like a centenarian's birthday cake, roll his eyes, and figure eight his head in excitement, quite pleased with himself.

At one point after the conversation slowed down and quiet eased into the room, Bernie looked pensive as he studied me in silence. "What is it, buddy, what are you thinking about?"

He paused through another silence. "You didn't forget me."

I choked down a long breath and stroked his buzzed head again. "Of course not, Bernie, I never forgot about you. I never forgot about you."

I then asked Bernie the question I had been privately phrasing since entering his room and seeing him prone.

"So, Bernie, the truth. How have you been, really?"

With no hesitation he answered, "Drifting."

"What do you mean?"

"Drifting," he answered again, but this time with a timbre that resonated deeply from within him before burrowing into me.

I looked at him closely, and for the first time that day I saw the beyond-middle-age Bernie Jones, the no-immediate-family-and-few-visitors Bernie Jones, the difficult-and-hard-to-handle Bernie Jones. I saw the never-to-be-forgotten Bernie Jones of a childhood long past and a promise finally kept. I saw Bernie Jones.

And as I watched him, I glimpsed the image of a single leaf on a barren tree, a leaf much like the one in O'Henry's short story. But this leaf finally does let go, flutters down into the languid waters of a minimal creek, and drifts slowly along the surface until being trapped by debris under a single-lane bridge. That was the drifting and entrapment I imagined Bernie Jones endured.

At 5:00 p.m. a nurse named Lisa brought Bernie his supper. We'd been together since early afternoon, and I felt I should leave them alone while he ate. I asked the nurse about visitors' hours, and she explained that visitors were permitted until 7:00 p.m., but since I had traveled so far, they could make an exception. I told Bernie I was going to leave for a while and asked if he needed anything.

"A puppy."

"What?"

"A puppy soft like Lady."

"Now, Bernie, you know you cannot have a pet," Nurse Lisa announced as much to me as to Bernie. I think she suspected I was going to go out and buy him a puppy, actually reading me pretty well, as only nurses can. "You know pets are not allowed."

"Phooey," Bernie huffed, the first time I had seen the agitated side of him. "Phooey," he repeated again just in case we had somehow missed his displeasure. And then, for good measure, a third "Phooey." He was making his point to both of us, but a kennel full of phooey was not going to produce a puppy.

I winked at Bernie and told him I'd be back in an hour.

"Promise?"

"Promise."

I stopped at the nurses' station to ask about Bernie's health and why he was in bed. The nurse told me that Bernie was permitted to be in his wheelchair for only one hour a day. He had developed a chronic spinal condition over the years and was now bedridden as a result, needing to be as flat and stretched out as possible. He was also diagnosed with a heart ailment that limited him exerting himself. Bernie was confined to bed for twenty-three hours a day.

I could not imagine Bernie without his wheelchair. The chair had been a companion his entire life, but now it sat alone except for one hour a day. When I was a kid, I felt sorry for him being in a wheelchair. As it turned out, the wheelchair years may have been his best years. How ironic is that?

I drove to Bellefontaine, the nearest location for a Wal-Mart, with a twofold mission: find something with Jeff Gordon's picture on it, and search the stuffed animal section for a soft and cuddly puppy. I had success, one of the few times in a Wal-Mart I was able to locate items on my own.

I was gone for over an hour, and when I returned to Heartland, the door to Bernie's room was closed. Hesitant to violate his privacy, I asked one of the nurses if I could go in, and she opened the door. The television was off and Bernie was awake, staring through the wall in front of him. I think he doubted my return. Disappointments pile up when life is reduced to a bed in a small, tidy, nursing home room.

"How was supper, Bernie?"

His head snapped toward me, face now grinning. "The same," he answered devilishly, "but always better when Lisa feeds me." Guys never change regardless of our age or condition.

His curiosity kicked in when he spotted the plastic Wal-Mart bag, and although he didn't ask about the contents, his focused look was question enough. I reached inside and pulled out a soft black-and-white puppy. She wasn't a Dalmatian like Lady, but the coloring was right. I set her beside Bernie's pillow.

"She isn't a real puppy, Bernie, but she's as good as I can do. I gave her a name if it's okay with you. What do you think about Second Lady?" His gums shined.

I adjusted Second Lady closer to his face and then cuddled the softness against his cheek. Bernie also liked the plastic, one-quart insulated Jeff Gordon thirst quencher with a built-in straw I bought for him. Yes, he liked the mug, but he loved Second Lady. One of these days I'm going to learn that sentimentality triumphs over practicality every day of the week.

We reminisced until after 9:00 p.m., and then the night nurse let me know I needed to leave with an unmistakable double tilt of her head toward the door. Neither of us wanted our day to end.

"Bernie, this has been a day for my memory book. What about you?"

"Yeah."

"Listen, I won't be able to visit you again for a while, but I'll come back, I promise. You know I'm promising that, right?" I watched his face for approval, and it finally came.

I rubbed his head once more and teased him by saying "Flattop," then walked away from his bed. As I reached the door, Bernie called out, "Good-bye, Rickie, my boy. Good-bye."

"Hey, Bernie, not good-bye. I'll see you again, I promise." He didn't say anything else.

I asked the night nurse if Bernie needed financial help, and she explained that all of his needs were being met. She also said that adjusting to nursing home life had been difficult for Bernie because he'd been raised in a real home with loving parents. She said he talked about DeGraff and me. I wanted to believe her.

I walked back to look in on him once more. His door was opened slightly, and Bernie was asleep with Second Lady by his head. As he slept, his arms and legs continued to dance involuntarily. Bernie's body could not rest even at rest. As I watched him, I wished I knew more about why he was like he was and how it felt to have no control over your own body or your own life. In those moments the complexities of my life disappeared.

I watched him for several minutes until, finally, I had seen enough.

I whistled during my drive back to Lima, something from Tchaikovsky and the Everly Brothers, I think. During the return flight to Little Rock, with eyes closed but not asleep, I remembered everything. And not wanting to forget even one insignificant detail, I remembered everything all over again. And again.

Who knows why we remember what we remember? Forget what we forget? Keep what we keep?

I know why.

REMEMBER ME

Remember me.

I have borne this life
with seldom tears
though often pained.
I rue those who live complaints.
My body, pretzel-shaped and salted,
bends stiffly
and threatens breaking.
My eyes are thick.
My gums are empty.
My head is smooth.
My legs have tripled.
I shuffle, wobble, teeter,
but seldom fall.
And as I look around me,
I see my semblances
shuffling, wobbling, teetering.
We mumble toward each other and nod.

At Christmas time
and Birthday time
we share each other's cards
and reminisce—
a son, a daughter,
now and then
a surprise great-grandchild.
Someone once
sent me a dozen oranges
and a pair of gray wool mittens.

Remember me.

XXII

Max Bernard Jones

Nine weeks after my visit with Bernie, I received a letter from Jinny Knief, our next-door neighbor in DeGraff, written in a perfectly neat cursive style that should be beyond the capability of a woman over ninety. The slender letter felt ominous in my hand, and hesitant to open it, I laid it aside. I had not received a letter from Jinny in years. Later, after everyone had gone home for the day and I was left alone in my campus office, I carefully slit the envelope open.

In all the years I've known Jinny Knief, she's never minced words, and this time she again cut straight to the point. Bernie died. He had suffered a heart attack and died two days later. Jinny explained she was sorry that no one contacted me, but they did not realize the gravity until it was too late. She wrote that Eunice Yoder attended the funeral and told her how peaceful Bernie looked in his casket.

Included in her letter was a clipped copy of *The Bellefontaine Examiner* obituary. It was extremely brief. His name in bold capital letters was the only thing standing out.

MAX BERNARD JONES

I guess Bernie's life wasn't much to write about. After reading the clip obituary, someone would think he hardly had a life at all.

I would have gone to his funeral. Because Bernie's life and mine were out of sync for so many years, I suppose the timing of me finding out about the funeral after it had occurred was to be expected. My timing is usually better. I cannot speak for Bernie's.

Several things haunt me yet today. The last time I saw Bernie his final word to me was good-bye, and that struck me as odd even then. In all our years of friendship, I do not remember us ever saying good-bye to one another. We usually said see you later or take it easy or good night. I am almost certain we never said good-bye. Even if he had no formal education and was confined to a wheelchair, Bernie Jones was always two steps ahead of me in how he anticipated things. I'm positive he sensed something the last time we were together.

I wish I had awakened him when I went back to his room. I don't know what more I might have said, but I wish I had awakened him. I would not have allowed good-bye to be his last word to me.

I wish I'd been at his funeral. Eunice Yoder said he looked peaceful. Bernie deserves to be at peace, and his spastic body deserves finally to be stilled. I think I deserve to have seen him that way. I think I deserved at least that much.

And I wish, these many years later, that Bernie and I could have ridden the Ferris wheel. That ride would have wheeled him through a lifetime of memories.

A Wished for Viewing

"It seems unfair that now you die."

> It's not too bad,
> Just kind of sad.
> So please don't cry,
> I said good-bye.

"And once at peace, how still you lie."

XXIII

Distance Means Nothing

Four decades is a long wait between one almost hug and the last. Sometimes I'm mad at myself for taking so long to visit Bernie, while other times I'm overwhelmingly relieved I saw him again before he died. The well-intended priorities of childhood often get misplaced during the journey through adulthood. But some of us are fortunate enough—and eventually mature enough—to recover past priorities. I think a predestined purpose for a memory keeper is to rediscover, to relive, and to retell, and then to help others in their rediscovering, reliving, and retelling. Those are nice gifts to share.

I still think about Bernie, although I never dream about him. I guess that is odd, but I suppose dreaming about him would be even odder. I wonder what he really thought about me and what other friendships he developed over the years. I would like to think that his truly memorable adventures were with me, but I'd be selfish to believe my paper route years were his best years.

I also wonder if Bernie learned anything from me, if he missed me, if he felt I had somehow let him down, and if, in fact, I had let him down. I wonder what went on in his life after I left DeGraff and continued on with my own.

Bernie Jones influenced my life, and I'm grateful for his influence. Having watched him live life in a wheelchair, with second-to-second spasms and contractions, helps me reduce the mundane inconveniences of everyday living to their proper insignificance. Bernie showed me how to live without complaining, and because of him, I see through the many people who complain without living. Because of him, I disregard all complainers.

Most of all Bernie showed me that simple is best, that common trumps complex. Although I needed several years to finally learn the lesson, I learned it well. When I knew him, Bernie's world was a wheelchair parked within an inconsequential side yard. Later his world existed in tidy, sterile, inconsequential nursing home rooms. Bernie lived a life of consequence within the inconsequential and seemed to know, long before I did, that simple worlds come to us and become us if we let them. Even in his drifting, I am certain he never really left.

We spend our lifetimes searching through worlds of complexity for a simplicity that is already waiting, patiently and almost in sight, within the borders of our own side yards. The beauty of a rainbow is not from where it is. No, the beauty is from where we are. Distance means nothing. Pots of gold wait, barely hidden, at our feet. Bernie Jones taught me that.

Yes, Bernie, my boy, between the two of us, you were the better teacher, the bigger influence. Thanks for being my side-yard superhero.

AND REMEMBER WHERE
THE RAINBOW HAD BEEN

If I could borrow anything
for just an hour,
I would borrow the rainbow
and promise to hold it
so very carefully.
And I would reach out
with both my hands
and my rainbow
and ask you to share it with me.
We would look at our rainbow
and talk,
and I could watch it
double
in your eyes.

Then,
after the rain,
and after our talk,
and after the rainbow
had faded from my hands,
I can still reach out
and smile back
and remember where the rainbow had been.

Postscript

When you lose a friend, you lose your memory sharer. You are now on your own. That makes you think a whole lot harder to try and keep the memories alive, to give them breath long after the breathing stops.

But memory keepers have an advantage. As we think, we remember even more...

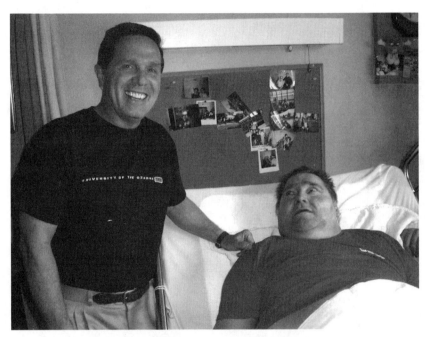

Rick "Rickie" Niece and Bernie Jones
HEARTLAND NURSING HOME